Also by J.I. Miller

The Book of Jims

Bills! Bills! Bills!

A Register of Wills & Williams,
Willys & Billys

J.I. Miller

authorHOUSE®

AuthorHouse™
1663 Liberty Drive
Bloomington, IN 47403
www.authorhouse.com
Phone: 833-262-8899

Published by AuthorHouse 11/19/2021

ISBN: 978-1-6655-4101-5 (sc)
ISBN: 978-1-6655-4099-5 (hc)
ISBN: 978-1-6655-4100-8 (e)

Library of Congress Control Number: 2021920806

William Tell   Buffalo Bill   William Shakespeare

William Penn   Bill Clinton   William the Conqueror

and various other bills

If you can't dazzle them with brilliance, baffle them with bullshit.
—William Claude Dunfield
(a.k.a. W.C. Fields)

I didn't always spell my name Bil. My parents named
me Bill, but when I started drawing cartoons on
the walls, they knocked the 'L' out of me.
—Bil Keane

I think I understand what military fame is; to be killed on the
field of battle and have your name misspelled in the newspapers.
—William Tecumseh Sherman

If you live long enough, you'll make mistakes.
—William J. Clinton

I don't make jokes. I just watch the government and report the facts.
—Will Rogers

If you can't make it good, at least make it look good.
—Bill Gates

Contents

To begin, begin.
—William Wordsworth

Bill Collection

Bills keep coming, ready or not. If you are not a William yourself, surely you know someone who is.

The name Bill, especially in the more formal form "William" is one of the most popular masculine names in English-speaking countries. During the medieval ages a full quarter of the guys in England were called William. We can blame that on William the Conqueror, the Norman Frenchman who introduced the name to England back in 1066. There were already a number of Williams in France. Two of them, William of St. Thierry and William of Conches, were 111h Century monks who spent their days—entire lifetimes of them—in silence, copying manuscripts from one sheet of vellum to another with a quill pen. These days that task is done in an instant by Xerox machines, so those monkish Williams have become superfluous, or as the Brits say, "made redundant." But unmonkish Williams proliferate today. In fact, some of the Williams you know are about as far from monkhood as could possibly be imagined.

The name William is derived from a Norman French name "Willaume," which, itself is derived from a German name "Willehelm." The "will" part of that means determination (as in "strong-willed;) the "helm" part refers to protection (as in "helmet.") Put those parts together and you get something that means "determined warrior" or "resolute protector." Sounds like a good sort of fellow to have around, right?

That probably accounts for why the name is so popular. The Social Security website tells us that for every hundred thousand people in America, precisely 888.94 of them are named William. There are 2,834,455 Williams living in America. But of course that number changes hourly as some Williams die off and others are born. The internet has several websites that parents expecting a baby boy can consult when looking around for a name to call the forthcoming kid. One site lists Liam, an Irish form of the name, at position #2 (after Oliver at #1.) William, in its pure form, comes in at #48. Another lists Liam at #1 and William at #3 (with Noah between them.) Yet another puts Noah in first place, followed by Liam at #2 and William at #5. A site showing names used for the last one hundred years shows William as the fifth most common, at least in English-speaking cultures. Go back an additional 300 years and it ranks 2nd. After John.

Don't look for Bills sitting around contemplating the universe in full lotus pose in Tibetan monasteries, kneeling and bowing in Syrian mosques, namaste-ing and ohm-ing on the ghats of the Ganges, or sitting at desks in the Althingi (Iceland's equivalent to a parliament thingy.). There won't be any Bills in the cast of a Noh drama or in the corps de ballet of the Ballet Russe. They will not be on the Carnivale samba floats of Rio nor among the lion dancers and dragon dancers of the Tet festivities in Viet Nam. Even in America it would be surprising to find very many Bills in the strawberry picking crews of central California, among the knife-juggling sous chefs of San Francisco's Chinatown, or doing a rain dance at a Navaho pow-wows. No, they are more likely to be found in more Anglo-Euro venues like rodeos, lacrosse tournaments, latte shops, and mosh pits. The name is, after all, of Anglo-Euro derivation.

Williams have been in the top ten since 2001 No matter how many sites are viewed, one concept emerges as clear: Williams abound. (William Shatner, William McKinley, William Shakespeare) But not all legally-named Williams are actually called "William." Liams do tend to be called exactly by their legal names—Liams, but Williams not so much. Sure, many of them, once old enough to sign their own names, use William in their official signature, but many of their friends, acquaintances, and second-cousins-twice-removed, call them something else, like Bill or Billy, Will or Willy.

All of those nicknames share an interesting common property: they are polysemic. Polysemic—that is the term for a word that has more than one meaning, like the word "left." Or, for that matter, the word "right." Consider the word Bill. As a proper noun it is a man's name (Bill Clinton, Bill Cosby, Bill Gates) or an act of Congress. Without the capital B, lower-case bills can be invoices that come in the mail, lists of things loaded onto a ship or a train, green pieces of paper in your wallet, or statements introduced to Congress before they are officially adopted.

Not a day on our lives goes by without us encountering some sort of lower-case b bill. Just pick up a newspaper and you will find reports of Congressional bills and Senate bills. Bills make headlines daily. We see headlines that, viewed as a series, sound like a biography of a guy named Bill:

BILL CONCEIVED THROUGH PROTESTS

BILL FAVORS BETTER PAY

LOCAL RESIDENTS FAVOR BILL

BILL INTRODUCED IN HOUSE

BILL STIMULATES LIVELY DISCUSSION

BILL LEAVES HOUSE

BILL FACES TOUGH OPPOSITION

BILL DIES IN SENATE

Note that this last headline could convey an entirely different meaning from:

BILL PASSES.

That one would mean one thing if it were on the front page, something else on the obituary page.

Wills, too, can be upper-cased for fellows' names (Will Smith, Will Ferrell, Will Rogers) or lower-cased to mean determination ("iron-willed,") a legal document explaining where somebody's worldly belongings should go following their demise, or wills can be wishes ("where there's a will.") Will can also be a verb—to will the grandfather clock to a grandson—or what grammarians call a "helper verb" indicating was **Billy The Kid**, nee Henry McCarty. And two of the Wills mentioned above are not really Wills— Will Smith's name is Willard and Will Ferrell's name is John. Go figure.

In the pages of this little Bill collection you will meet lots of Williams. It is indeed a register of Wills. "Register of wills"—if that title has a familiar ring to it that is because the last time you participated in a local election there were probably "down ballot" candidates who were running for the office, a "row" office called Register of Wills. When medical interviewers perform tests for cognitive ability—testing whether your brain is functioning properly—there are often questions like "What day is today?", "Can you tell me where we are?", or "Who is President of the United Sates?" Chances are, assuming you are not experiencing cognitive impairment, you can answer all three of those questions.

But what if they asked you, and thank God they don't, "Who is Register of Wills in this county?"

Your likely response: "Duh."

You probably cannot name your Register of Wills any more than you can name your County Coroner nor your Prothonotary. Or what if they asked you (they won't) "What does your Register of Wills do?"

Your initial response: "Duh."

But on further cognition about it you might come up with something like, "Well, I guess he writes registers the wills. You know, writes them down."

Job descriptions for Registers of Wills vary from county to county, but one thing they do *not* do is write down the wills. You cannot just assume that your grandmother's will—that document which will settle family arguments about who gets the grandfather clock or the diamond ring—is on file in a government office. The job descriptions usually do include other tasks like probating wills and collecting estate taxes. So here you have it: Death and Taxes. Like Bills, whether upper case or lower, you cannot avoid them.

Among the Wills, Williams, Bills, and Willies you will find here are guys of all stripes. Yes, they are all guys; no women allowed. That, of course, leaves out singer Billie Holliday, tennis ace Billie Jean King, and other women with cajones to go through life carrying a name clearly associated with the opposite gender. Some Bills are clearly recognized as Good Guys; some are the Other Kind. Some you have heard of; some you have not. Some are living; some are not. Some are famous for something they did. Some are not famous at all, even though they made significant contribution to society.

An excellent example of a William in that last category is **William Dunbar**, a sixteenth century Scottish poet in the court of William IV. His significant contribution to society happened in 1503: He was the first person, at least the first one in a kilt, to publish the word *fuck*.

William the Conker

There'll always be an England; there always was. And there were always kings; some of them were queens. Most of the really early kings had unpronounceable Game of Thrones names like Athelstan, Harthacnut, Unraed, or Eadwig. But that all changed in the year 1066, when the first of several kings named William came in. He did not start out as English at all.

Because he led what we call the Norman invasion and Normans lived in northern France, we think of him as French. But he wasn't French either; he was Danish. Not only Danish, but a Viking to boot. Had he been French his name would have been Guillaume. Had he been Persian, Wallam. Or, if from certain parts of Italy, Cuglierme. But in Danish — the language that gives us complicated words and phrases like "Tillykke med fødselsdagen" when they want to wish you a happy birthday or "Jeg vil gerne kysse dine bryster" when they want to kiss your breasts—the word for "William" is simply: William

The first thing he did when he made it across the channel and landed on an English beach was to eat a mouthful of sand. We have no idea why he did this, but he didn't like it, spat it out in disgust, and thus began a long-standing tradition of labeling English food as not very good.

His army of Vikings had names with lots of G's in them—names like Godhardt, Gunnlaugur, and Gyrd. Those Viking G's were not the soft, gentle G's of "gingivitis", "Georgia" or "genitalia" but were the hard, clunky G's of "gargoyle", "gargantuan" or "gorgonzola". And their style of battle was not the subtle, intellectual competition of *The Seventh Seal* but the more macho *Braveheart* kind. In 1066 there were no remote-controlled weapons, no ICMB's, no drones nor robots. Fighting was up close and personal, *Gladiator* style. There was lots of metal-to-metal clashing, lots of twirling of maces and slashing of swords, lots of clanging and clonking. When it came to bashing heads and smashing skulls William apparently excelled. That is why the William of The Battle of Hastings became known as William the Conker.

He was also known as **William the Bastard**, because his archetypical Viking father was not married to his archetypical French mistress.

A remarkable thing about the Battle of Hastings is that it is recorded forever in a very curious way—on a lengthy piece of linen known as the Bayeux Tapestry, approximately the length of three swimming pools and the width of a dinner napkin. It really is not a tapestry at all but, technically, it is a work of embroidery. It was commissioned by William's half-brother Odo, which is also very curious since William kept Odo locked up in prison most of the time, and stitched by William's wife and her ladies-in-waiting. Images in it document the entire battle—the buildup of arms, the construction of boats, hundreds of horses and dead or dying humans—the whole of it, even including an image of Halley's Comet, whose most celebrated appearance was in the year 1066.

The second thing he did was to take inventory of everything and everybody in his newly vanquished England and record it all in the Doomsday Book. What is especially important about that book has nothing to do with any literary eloquence nor elaborate medieval calligraphy but that in its content he made it dogmatically clear that everything and everybody basically belonged to him—every hill, every ditch, every young maiden, every serf. Of course there were middle managers given titles like dukes and earls, but there was no question that, all things considered, He da Man.

Apparently his disgust of English cuisine had abated, for during his twenty-one years on the throne he became fatter and fatter. While fighting in France he fell off his steed and was trampled to death. They buried him, with difficulty, right there on the spot. The difficulty was that his body was too fat to fit into the hole they had dug, so part of it stuck out.

Even though William himself was born a bastard, he and his wife had ten thoroughly legitimate children together. Four of them succumbed to the perils of infancy and childhood and three of the surviving ones were girls. That left three sons to share his inheritance. The oldest son was given Normandy and the youngest son was given money. The middle one, who was his favorite, or as the Brits would have it—his favourite—got stuck with England. He had himself crowned immediately, causing his father to acquire yet another nickname. He became known ever since as William I, now that there was a William II.

The second William was called **William Rufus** because of his reddish, or rufous complexion. Considering the relatively low number of sunny days in England this was probably due to genetics rather than sunburn. Or maybe he was just angry. He was as Viking as his father where battles were involved and he ruled ruthlessly for thirteen years until he was shot by an arrow while hunting in the New Forest. History is still debating whether it was an accident or an assassination, possibly organized by his younger brother. Since he had never married there were no heirs, at least no legitimate ones. And when inheritance of a throne was involved, legitimacy mattered big time. So the throne passed to the third son of William (William the Conqueror aka William the Bastard or William I.) This was the son mentioned above who was given money instead of a crown, the possible assassinator. His name was Henry and we know him today as Henry I.

Following those two early Williams, England had to wait nearly six hundred years for another. In the meantime there were several King Edwards, eight King Henrys, a couple of Jameses, one Elizabeth, a Mary, and lots of fuss about boundaries and religion, lots of sibling rivalries, occasional beheadings, and little improvement in cuisine.

The third William, or in proper Roman numerals, William III, came to the throne in a curious way: he was invited! The situation in England in 1688 was complicated, but the gist of it was that people were fed up with their current king, James II, and wanted something better—something better than a power-hungry, me- firster, and definitely somebody who wasn't Catholic. He had a daughter named

Mary who was Protestant. Parliament and the nobles wanted Mary instead of her father, so they invited a Netherlander named **William of Orange**, who happened to be a nephew of James, to organize and army and come over to depose James. By all rights and traditions Mary (perhaps of Grapefruit) should take the throne, but she was not truly keen on the idea so Parliament suggested that she marry William, the conquering hero. She was fifteen at the time and not truly keen on the marriage idea either. She wept during the ceremony. The marriage was motivated by political forces more than by affection and he maintained a bevy of mistresses on the side. Thus, with this marriage, William was instrumental in deposing the man who was his uncle and his father-in-law.

So Parliament got their Mary as queen but William, the man of the house, had all the power. People liked Mary even though she was unassertive and somewhat of a wimp. They didn't really like William but he seemed to be able to get things done. Parliament worked out a compromise that specified they should rule jointly. Hence, William and Mary. She died of smallpox five years into the reign and William ruled alone for eight more years.

He became sickly and asthmatic and moved away from downtown London to the "country," which was Hampton Court. But during the time of their reign British explorers were claiming land all over the world. That is why so many sites, cities, even ships and colleges have William or Mary in their names—like Williamstown, Williamsburg, the Queen Mary and the Queen Mary 2, or the College of William and Mary.

Fast forward a hundred and twenty-eight years to 1831, skipping over four King Georges and one Queen Anne to the next King William, **William IV**. As King Williams go, this one was the least exciting. His father was King George III, who was declared insane, and he succeeded his brother George IV, who showed some of the same symptoms. He had at least two nicknames: "The Sailor King" because he had been sent off to the Royal Navy when he was thirteen, and "Silly Billy" because of his tendency to give rambling speeches and spontaneous, unreasoned comments. Sort of like some Tweets of some government officials today.

In his seven years sitting on the throne he did not produce any earth-shaking legacies; he was more productive in his bed, participating in the conception of quite a lot of offspring. He lived much of his life with an actress who bore him ten illegitimate children. Later, he agreed to marry a German princess for political reasons and they had four totally legitimate children but none survived infancy. He came to the throne at age sixty-four, the oldest of any British monarch to do that. When he died of a heart attack at seventy-one with no legitimate heirs, he was succeeded by his niece who called him Uncle Billy. He probably called her Vicky. We call her Victoria.

The next time England has a King William he will be known as **William V**, but that might be a long way off because, for one thing, his grandmother Elizabeth, in her nineties, is still Queen. When she is done, if that indeed ever happens, her oldest son Prince Charles is next in line. Most folks know about Charles because on July 29, 1981, he costarred in a lavish, globally televised royal wedding with Princess

Diana Spencer. Together, as Duke and Duchess of Wales, their every sneeze, every public appearance, every private quarrel, was World News.

They had two little boys, William and Harry. As the elder, it is **Prince William** who is at present second in line to be King. His full name is William Arthur Philip Louis Mountbatten-Windsor, aka the Duke of Cambridge. Diana, his mummy, did what she could to provide a "normal" childhood for the boys, taking them to amusement parks and the like, but anything approaching "normalcy" is a stretch when royalty is involved. At the age of nine William was struck on the forehead by an uncontrolled golf club and still has a scar. He calls it his "Harry Potter scar" because, he claimed as a child, it sometimes glows. When he was even younger he, like many other lads of his age, said he wanted to be a policer officer, a Bobby, when he grew up. His little redheaded brother Harry, apparently comprehending their unique situation in life, said, "Oh, no you can't. You've got to be King."

It is an awful thing to wish upon a kid. But like it or not, he is stuck with it and there is little he can do to get out of it. He can't even abdicate "to marry the woman he loves" as his great-great uncle did because he has already married her. Where earlier kings battled their siblings, their cousins, and their aunts for the privilege of taking the throne, more recent royalty would probably be glad to be rid of it. However, William has done admirably in accepting his fate. His mum died in an accident when he was fifteen. He had an okay university career at St. Andrews and saw military service in the Royal Air Force, and he has done more than his share of appearances at ribbon-cuttings, ship christenings and the like. But his real fame came when, like his father's did at his own royal wedding to Princess Diana, he married gorgeous Kate Middleton in 2011. There is nothing like a fairy tale wedding to keep people glued to their tellies. Because of the time difference between Westminster Abbey and any place in North America, New World wedding watchers set their alarms for awakenings as early as 2:00 a.m. When the whole thing was over they could go back to bed, go to work, go to school, or otherwise go on about the business of their lives however they want. But the royals, William especially, have their work cut out for them. They have to be royal. That means William's gotta be King.

Eventually. Maybe. Probably. One thing is certain: little Prince Billy will never be a Bobby.

*My definition of an intellectual is someone who can listen to the
William Tell Overture and not think of the Lone Ranger.*
—*Sir Billy Connoly*

The Tell Tale Told

A simple test; it will not take long: list three things you know about **William Tell**. Take as much time as you need, like, probably, one half of one minute.

Now, assuming that you have not cheated by Googling or Binging, you probably have two entries. One is something about *The Lone Ranger* and the other is something about shooting an apple of a little boy's head while wearing lederhosen. That is likely pretty much it.

Let's start with that Overture bit. You may have heard the old joke "Where does the Lone Ranger take his trash?" The answer: "Ta da dump, ta da dump, ta da dump, dump, dump." And when you say those words, chances are good that you fall into a rhythmic pattern known in music as a cabaletto. The term is derived from a word meaning "horse" and refers to that short "gallopy gallopy," "giddayup giddayup" form. Trumpet players need to be accomplished double-tonguers to play it well, because it is really fast, prestissimo.

If you know the tune at all it is probably because of *The Lone Ranger*, but if you are on the younger side of seventy you might not know who he is. Or was. Well, he originated early in the 1930's as a radio hero and then in the 40's and 50's morphed into a television staple. He was a Texas Ranger, an archetypical good guy who wore a black eyemask and fought quintessential bad guys. He rode a horse named Silver. At the end of each episode, having saved the Old West from yet another Evil-of-the-Week, he rode off into the sunset commanding to his horse, "Hi, ho, Silver, away" leaving bystanders, passersby, and onlookers aghast and wondering, "Who was that masked man?"

But the Lone Ranger was hardly a loner. He had a sidekick Potawatomi friend named Tonto usually riding his horse Scout beside him. It is not entirely clear what, since the Potawatomis were from the Upper Peninsula of Michigan, Tonto was doing in the middle of Comanche territory in Texas, but we do know that a frequent expression of his was "I seek justice, kemo sabe." So he must have ended up in Texas as a result of some real or perceived injustice somewhere in his past. But "kemo sabe" is still an enigma. Some say it is Comanche for "trusty scout. Others say "faithful friend." Or "white shirt." And since it isn't too far from the Spanish *quien sabe* it could even mean "who knows?" Who really knows? Who really cares?

And during all of this the musicians in the background are double-tonguing that cabaletto from William Tell Overture. An Overture, something played before something bigger. In this case the bigger thing is a four act opera. A really big one. Some performances take five hours. Gioachino Rossini, the lone arranger, wrote the thing in 1829. He had already written some thirty-eight other operas, including a few big hits such as *The Italian in Algiers* and *The Barber of Seville* (think "Figaro,

Figaro, Figaro"), but it was *William Tell* that caused him to pack it in. He never wrote another opera as long as he lived, another forty more years.

The Overture itself is even long. Twelve full minutes. That's before the curtain even opens for Act I. The Overture is in four parts: a slow, hopeful Dawn, an expressive Storm, a very peaceful and pastoral Call to the Cows. As musical pastorals go it hardly ever gets more pastoral than this. The flutes bring to mind shepherds on the hillsides. Those hills are alive. So much so that you can just feel that sunshine on your shoulders. Just see those cattle grazing on the edelweiss. Just smell that dairy air!

But it is the last movement, the rousing finale March of the Swiss Soldiers, that we are familiar with. It is hard to imagine The Lone Ranger drumming up much interest with Call to the Cows. But *kemo sabe*, who knows?

Now let's look at that bit about the apple and the lederhosen. There is no documented historical evidence for William Tell at all, but the legend is as strong as ever. It happened way back once upon a time in the early edge of the 1300's in a small village called Altforf in a valley at the southern end of Lace Lucerne in a canton called Uri in what is now called Switzerland. On the other side of the Alps, in Austria, the Hapsburg Empire was thriving and was desirous of expanding. The Austrians sent a rough, strutting, bullying bailiff named Hermann Gessler to Altdorf to bring the Altdorfians under the Hapsburg yoke.

There was no subtlety about this Gessler; he insisted that everyone recognize his authority. He stuck his hat, appropriately decorated with ostentatious peacock feathers, on top of a pole in the center square of the village and demanded that everyone who passed by it should bow to it. Not quite everyone did. William Tell didn't.

Since he made his living as a chamois hunter it is possible that he had been out in the mountains hunting when the word went out about katowing to that hat and he might not have even known that he was supposed to. Or perhaps he was thoroughly aware of the order but chose to defy it. For whatever reason, he did not bow before Gessler's hat and was caught in the non-act and arrested by Gessler's men. Gessler made a deal with Tell: he was ordered to shoot an apple off his son Walter's head with his chamois-hunting crossbow. If successful, he would be freed. If he failed he would die (as, obviously, so would his son.) If he refused to try it he would be killed also.

Gessler probably figured that the likelihood of Tell hitting a target the size of an apple was about equal to the likelihood of finding an edelweiss flower blooming in a desert. But, confident in his crossbow skill, Tell allowed his son (who is called Jemmy in the opera; (*kemo sabe* why)) to be tied up to a pole and an apple was placed on his head. Tell put an arrow in his crossbow and another in the quiver on his back. Then he took aim, released the arrow, and in an instant—splat—the apple was gone from his son's head. The crowd cheered. This pissed Gessler off. He asked Tell what the second arrow was for and learned that it was meant for him in case he missed the apple and killed his son. Further pissed, Gessler had Tell arrested again and sentenced him to life in the dungeons of a castle on a distant shore of Lake Lucerne.

A bit of geography is important here. If you look at a map of Lake Lucerne you immediately see that it would be very easy to get lost on it, for its outline is contorted like the lower intestines and bowels of the human digestive tract. Navigating by colonoscopy might be more effective than by compass.

On the trip to the dungeons, with Tell shackled in chains, a fierce storm blew up and the oarsmen got lost somewhere in the sigmoid colon. But our hero William Tell, who knew the lake quite well, was released to guide the boat to a cove that he knew about. When the boat drew near the shore he leaped out and landed on a flat rock, now called the *Tellsplatte* where Tell apparently landed with a splat, and pushed the boat out into the storm with Gessler and his crew in it. Tell, with that second arrow still in his quiver, snuck around in the dark and waited near the dock where he knew Gessler's little boat would eventually arrive. When the boat pulled up Tell shot Gessler through the heart— splat—as cleanly as he had shot the apple of his son's head and thereby saved the canton of Uri from Hapsburg oppression.

Whether William Tell was a hero, a rebel, a terrorist or a murderer matters little. He is credited with saving Switzerland from Hapsburg oppression and Austrian rule. That pole in the town square of Altdorf with that peacock-feathered hat has been replaced by a bronze statue of Tell and his son. Both are wearing lederhosen. The *Tellsplatte* rock on the eastern shore of Lake Lucerne is enshrined in a columned pavilion somewhat resembling the one housing our own Plymouth Rock.

Heroes like Tell abound as symbols for political and individual freedom. Scandinavians have their Beowulf, the French have Joan of Arc, the English have Guy Fawkes, the Scots have Robert the Bruce, and Protestants everywhere have Martin Luther. Even Texans have their own Davy Crockett. We don't really know whether William Tell was real or not, but we do know for certain that the hills are alive in Switzerland and it is free.

And we do have that Overture. Ta da dump. Ta da dump.

Let the people think they govern and they will be governed.
—William Penn

Billy Penn

William Penn, America's first real estate developer, wore a black hat.

It was not the black hat of bad guys in westerns, but the good guy black hat of the smiling gentleman on every box of Quaker Oats, the black hat of every kid portraying a Pilgrim in a Thanksgiving pageant, or the black hat worn by pretty much every male in seventeenth century American colonies. William Penn himself has come down through history with basically favorable reviews and is generally regarded as a good guy. That cannot be said, however, about some of the other Williams who came before or after him, many of whom were his own relatives.

Most Americans with even the slightest interest in history or geography learn somewhere in their schooling that the state name of Pennsylvania, or technically, the Commonwealth of Pennsylvania, means "Penn's woods" and is named for William Penn. Few folks, though, know that the William Penn of the state—sorry, of the Commonwealth—is not the William Penn we think of as ours. No, not *"our"* William Penn but that of his father, also named William Penn, **Sir William Penn.**

The way it happened was that William Penn, our father who wert in England, was a wealthy member of the privileged class and admiral in the British navy. At one point he lent 16,000 pounds to King Charles II for assistance with some wars—no small sum, considering that those 16,000 pounds would be worth about four million dollars in today's currency and would have purchasing power of a quarter of a billion. After father William Penn's death son William Penn, *our* William Penn, asked the king to return the money. King Charles, not having that kind of cash stashed in a corner of his castle, gave him land in America instead. Trouble was, it really wasn't his to give away; it was already occupied by Indians. At least that is what Christopher Columbus called the natives encountered when he hit land because he figured he was landing in India.

The Charter for Pennsylvania was given to Billy Penn on March, 4, 1681 and he immediately appointed a Bill, his first cousin **William Markham**, as governor. Meanwhile Penn, who, back in England with his Quakerish beliefs and actions had been in out of prisons—solid, hulking structures like the Tower of London and Newgate Prison— much of his young life, was eager to sail to the New World and set up a Holy Experiment. By 1682 he had his affairs in sufficient order to sail with a few other Quakers to Pennsylvania on the Welcome. The Indians, however, probably did not share welcoming enthusiasm.

They must have been pleasantly surprised when they discovered that this white fellow in that weird black hat was actually a good guy. Instead of getting off the boat and immediately start slashing their throats and burning their lodgings as many other European arrivers had done, he sat with them in the shade of a giant oak tree and had a discussion with them. Not only did he treat the natives with respect and even learn their languages but he also actually paid them for their lands—and paid a fair price! He never tried to cheat them.

The next generation of Penns, however, was not so kind, at least where real estate was concerned. Penn, *our* William Penn, had purchased lands approximately thirty or so miles north of what is now Philadelphia. By 1737 his three sons had blown through their inheritance and began selling northern lands that had never been truly purchased from the natives. In an effort to give an outward appearance of fairness, although inwardly deceitful, they made an agreement to purchase as much land within a perimeter prescribed "as a man could go in a day and a half." The agreement was known as The Walking Purchase and the walk itself as The Great Walk.

Everyone assumed that actual walking would be involved. But, no, the Penn boys hired professional runners and even cleared a trail through the woods a day before to make the "walking" go farther and faster. So the Indians were cheated out of 12,000 square miles of woodlands that had been their territory forever. The trio of young Penns then sold off chunks of land to arriving Europeans at considerable profit to themselves. These actions, far from their father's Quaker ideals, would have been appalling to their father. History does not regard them as good guys.

There is an interesting land-grabbing story about another one of Penn's governors named Bill: **Sir William Keith**. Sir William, from Scotland, was appointed by Penn as deputy governor of the colony of Pennsylvania in 1716. While reviewing the financial records of the government preceding him he noticed that some funds were missing. The previous treasurer was deceased, so Sir William approached family survivors of the dead debtor in Philadelphia to recover the funds.

"We don't have that kind of money," said the treasurer's family "but we do have a 1200 acre farm sixteen miles north of the city."

"Fine. I'll take it," said Keith.

That first person pronoun is significant. Note that he did not say "we" as in "We, the people of the colony of Pennsylvania will take it," but "I will take it." And with that he acquired 1200 acres of Pennsylvania woodlands for himself. To make it appear legitimate and beneficial for the commonfolk he had the lands cleared for fields and planted rye and barley with the intent of establishing a distillery to produce single malt scotch. This was, of course, going to raise revenue for the colony. Yeah, right.

The operation involved nearly ninety servants, most of them indentured immigrants from Germany but also a few slaves. One of them, called, simply, **Will** ran away. The ad in the *Pennsylvania Gazette* offering a five pounds reward for his return described him as

"A MOLATTO SLAVE, NAMED WILL, ABOUT 29 YEARS OF AGE, APPROACHING VERY NEAR THE NEGROE COMPLEXION, BEING OF A NEGROE FATHER, AND INDIAN MOTHER .... ABOUT FIVE FEET EIGHT INCHES .... COUNTENANCE SOMEWHAT PITTED WITH THE SMALL-POX .... SPEAKS BOTH ENGLISH AND DUTCH .... A VERY CUNNING, SENSIBLE FELLOW"

In 1746 an ad like that was as routine then as a notice of a weekend garage sale is today, but now, nearly three centuries later, that short ad about the missing Will gives us hints of prevailing attitudes and conditions of the earlier day—the value of the worker based on his physique, ownership, the attitude toward mixed races, and the diseases. It is also interesting that Will had only one name—no family name— just Will. According to birth records his father was also Will—only Will. This was very common among enslaved populations, where single names like Moses, Toby, and Will were prevalent. Owners named their slaves the same way they named their dogs and their cows—Rover, Rex, and Rascal or Bossie, Buttercup, and Blossom. A last name was not needed; the default was that of the Master.

It was generally assumed that Will had fled to New York and ships' captains were put on lookout for him, but he was found near Philadelphia and returned to the barley farm. Unlike the violent treatment of runaways depicted in TV series and movies, the punishment imposed was relatively light. The Master was glad to have Will—cunning, sensible Will—back. There was work to be done.

With all of those ninety-odd helpers Sir William built a stone mansion with nine rooms equally distributed among three floors; it was a charming little weekend cabin for himself and his family to escape the city.

Although Sir William was hired as governor by William Penn, he was fired nine years later by Mrs. William Penn. He, once a wealthy colonial landowner, died an ignominious death in debtors' prison in London. His barley farm mansion still exists as a Pennsylvania State Historic Site called Graeme Park, named for a subsequent owner, in the suburbs north of Philadelphia.

At least two other landmarks still exist from Penn's time in Philadelphia, Pennsylvania. One is Philadelphia, Pennsylvania, itself. When Penn landed there in 1682 he counted a dozen or so log structures. He envisioned something bigger. The site along the Delaware River (named for Baron de La Warr, an early explorer of the area) extends two miles west to another river, the unpronounceable, unspellable, unpotable, and barely navigable Schuylkyll (which means "hidden river" in Dutch). Penn drew out a river-to-river gridwork plan for the city. He intended it to become a "greene country towne" with grassy areas and orchards surrounding all of the buildings, for he had experienced the epic fires of seventeenth century London and wanted to design a fireproof city. The plan included five grassy open squares, four of which were scattered towards the corners out from a large central one. They still remain.

The central square originally housed a fountain where folks would carry their oaken buckets to obtain water for the necessities of living. Eventually, that was replaced with City Hall, a magnificent Second Empire structure housing the current government of Philadelphia, Pennsylvania. At its very top is a magnificent dome and farther atop that is a thirty-seven foot statue of William Penn himself. For years nothing could be built in the city any higher than the top of Billy Penn's black hat at 548 feet above Market Street. To build anything high would bring on the "curse of Billy Penn" and no Philadelphia sports team would win a championship. However, the Phillies won the World Series in 1980 and 2008, the Eagles won the Super Bowl in 2018, and the Flyers won the Stanley Cup two years in a row in the mid 1970's.

Billy Penn stood there as the highest thing in the city until 1987 when a skyscraper called One Liberty Place was constructed. The tallest building in Philadelphia now is the Comcast Technology Center at 1,121 feet—a little less than a quarter of a mile high. Anything that much higher than Billy Penn's hat down on the top of City Hall would doom Philly teams forever. So a teensy replica of the original statue was bolted on the highest steel beams of the building at the end of 2017. It's only four inches high. The Eagles made it into the play-offs but didn't make it to the Super Bowl that winter.

Even today Bill Penn stands up there atop the City Hall dome in his waistcoat and frock coat looking down over his "city of brotherly love."

The odd thing about Billy Penn, though is what he is doing, or at least what it looks like he is doing. In public no less! Supposedly he has extended his hand out just below waist level as a blessing for the city below. But when the side of his hand is viewed from a major avenue from the northwest it appears that he has taken a serious dose of Viagra, has whipped it out, and his holding his own. Ads for Viagra warn that if the condition persists for longer than four hours medical help is necessary. Poor Billy Penn has been this way since 1894 when the statue was, well, erected.

He is cleaned every ten years and the process takes many months, so most of the time he is in scaffolding. And Philadelphia, Pennsylvania, with a population of more than a million and a half, now has a dozen or so skyscrapers towering well above Billy Penn's hat. The "greene country towne" is now mostly paved over and every once in a while fires do occur. But the grid plan of the city still prevails and the open squares still offer serenity. Billy Penn still stands erect, but tourists do not stand in forty-minute queues to take selfies with him. That honor goes to Rocky. He can be found—where else?—at the steps of the art museum.

But Billy Penn is still up there and still holding his own.

Bison Bill

Before there were Ringling Brothers, before Barnum and Bailey, before *Cirque du Anything*, there was *Buffalo Bill's Wild West*.

William Frederick Cody, a.k.a. **Buffalo Bill**, was an Iowa boy by birth and, like all boys from Iowa and practically everywhere else, played Cowboys and Indians with great enthusiasm and fantasy. You know—Shoot-'em-up, bang, bang!—but all in pretend. Immediately upon reaching puberty he headed further westward into the real Wild West country we associate him with. He was on his way to Colorado in 1859 aspiring to strike it rich in the Pikes Peak Gold Rush when he saw an ad seeking "skinny, expert riders willing to risk death daily." The strike-it-rich bit didn't pan out for him, so he answered the ad. Typically, as fourteen-year old he thought this sounded more exciting than threatening and he became a rider for the Pony Express. Eventually, but still in his youth, he fought for the Yankee side in the Civil War and later served as a civilian scout for the United States Army. He also did time as a trapper, as a wagon master, and as a stagecoach driver.

At one point he had a contract to supply buffalo meat to workers on the Kansas Pacific Railroad and he killed more than four thousand buffalo in a year and a half. Another fellow named Bill, one **William Comstock**, had a similar contract and their buddies soon began to call them both by the same nickname, "Buffalo Bill." Realizing that only one of them should hold title to that moniker they held a contest. Whichever one could kill the most buffalo in an eight hour day was to be Buffalo Bill forever. The other was to live ignominiously in shame as just plain Bill.

The contest results:

William Cody 68

William Comstock 48

So Cody became Buffalo Bill, but the name is technically inaccurate. The Bill part is okay since lots of guys named William are called "Bill" but the Buffalo part is imprecise because there really were not any true buffaloes roaming in the American West at all. True buffalo are animals that live in central and southern Africa (*Syncerus caffer,* the Cape Buffalo) or the water buffalo (*Bubalus bubalis)* of Asia. The giant shaggy creatures of the American west, the ones so famously roaming in those homes on the ranges, the ones that appeared on US nickels from 1913 to 1938, the ones that even today can cause a three-mile traffic jam when even a single one is spotted munching ever so nonchalantly on a sagebrush anywhere in Yellowstone National Park, the ones that produced the hides for Native American clothing and rugs for the great rooms of yuppie ski lodges—they're not buffalo at all. They are bison. *Bison bison*. But somehow "Bison Bill" doesn't cut it.

He real claim to fame and fortune came from show business. That's where he found the gold that escaped him at Pikes Peak. There's no business like show business. There had always been rodeos in the west, local events where cowboys competed to see who was best at roping cows or riding broncos, but there was nothing of the circus-type spectacle that Cody introduced in 1873 as an enterprising thirty-seven year old. *"Buffalo Bill's Wild West"* was extravagant. The world had never seen anything like it. The greatest show on earth. At its peak it traveled with a cast and crew of more than five hundred people that included more than a hundred American Indians, a few people of color, and even some token women. The menagerie included hundreds of horses used both for riding and for pulling things around. There were also thirty buffalo, or, well, *Bison*. Every living thing, whether two-legged or four-legged, needed to be fed three times a day. That required advance coordination in every city visited to arrange for purchase and preparation of food. The show transported bleachers to seat up to twenty thousand spectators and enough canvas to cover them. The performance area itself, though, was open to the sky. That was probably a good thing considering all the dust kicked up by all the whooping and hollering, shooting and shouting, and stomping and stampeding that went on during the performance. Train travel for the entire show required more than fifty railroad cars.

The shows themselves had a theme that changed each year, but they were generally fanciful reenactments of western events—Custer's Last Stand, The Great Stagecoach Robbery, Pioneer Pony Express Ride, and lots of variations of what could generically be lumped as grown-up, choreographed versions of "Cowboys and Indians" that Cody and his buddies had played as kids in their Iowa backyards.

At various stages in its history *Buffalo Bill's Wild West Show* featured several of the era's most widely celebrated celebrities—like the sharpshooter Martha Jane Cannary ("Calamity Jane"), Annie Oakley (another sharpshooter), and "Wild" Bill Hickok. Real live Indians were a big hit and one of the biggest draws was Chief Sitting Bull himself. He was paid fifty dollars a week just to ride around the arena one time during each performance.

Cody shipped the whole show over to England for a command performance before Queen Victoria. Being a command performance, nobody got paid. But it was not a financial disaster because it generated enough interest sell two and a half million tickets to three hundred subsequent shows. That averages out to be about eight thousand tickets per performance. Think of the logistics for handling the crowds—the "car parks" for the horses and carriages, the portable loos, the technical aspects of the production. After England they toured the Continent eight times, leaving a trail of horse manure and buffalo chips such as Europeans had never seen before. They also performed the show in Outer Mongolia and then, back home, at the Chicago World's Fair of 1893. Without any competition other than what a few smaller mimicking shows could offer, the show was a runaway hit for more than three decades and Cody, wisely, switched to making movies.

Once the show was a success, he purchased a plot of land along the North Platte River in North Platte, Nebraska, as a location to build a mooring place of relaxation from his travels and to please his second wife. (He had divorced his first wife after learning that she tried to poison his coffee.) He called it Scout's Rest. Maps of Nebraska and signs along I-70 call it Buffalo Bill's Ranch. And it is indeed a restful place. The house is a shingled affair built in Second Empire style and there area few outbuildings, including a large stable full of carriages and saddles. In all of those various spaces a variety of Buffalo Bill relics are displayed— things like show posters, lots of rifles, uniforms, medals, and buffalo robes. There are also flicky, scratchy film clips of actual *Wild West* performances. Probably the most bizarre objects in the collection are a necklace made of human hair and the teeth of Isham, his favorite horse.

The Buffalo Bill legacy is expansive. He founded Cody, Wyoming, near the east entrance to Yellowstone National Park. A major attraction there is the Buffalo Bill Center of the West, a modern complex of five museums and a research library. The museums have something for everyone, from visitors interested in western art to Second Amendmenters interested in firearms and to kids who want to see Indian stuff and dinosaurs. One museum is dedicated to Buffalo Bill himself.

One of the largest, in terms of drawing power, legacies of Buffalo Bill is the NFL team that bears his name. They play in New Era Stadium near Buffalo, New York, that seats more than 71,000 fans in permanent seating. That is about four times the size of those portable bleachers Cody hauled around for his Wild West shows. And it has flush toilets. Cody had nothing to do with the city or the football team. The town was named for a nearby stream, the Buffalo Creek, which was named by French fur traders. Apparently a few herds of *Bison bison* occasionally roamed that far east. But if it were not for the celebrity and legendhood of Buffalo Bill, the football team could have been called the Buffalo Wings, the Buffalo Rugs, the Buffalo Robes, the Buffalo Burgers, or the Buffalo Anythings. But "Buffalo Bills," besides being alliterative, captures the desired image of a stampeding, hulking powerhouse that fits football. A true American buffalo weighs 1400 pounds; an average Buffalo Bill weighs only 180. So it is somewhat self-aggrandizing for the team to compare themselves with the real thing.

There is no opera about William Cody as there is about William Tell, but there is a wonderful American musical—*Annie Get Your Gun*, by Irving Berlin. The plot is a bit corny as it revolves around two performers in *Buffalo Bill's Wild West* who fall for each other but are damned if either will let the other know it at least until the end of Act II. It is the show that gave us the songs *Doin' What Comes Naturally, The Girl That I Marry, Anything You Can Do,* and the most-heard tune from the show, clearly the brashest, *There's No Business Like Show Business.* The *No Business* song was used in the finale of the original Broadway version that opened in 1946 and ran for 1,147 performances with Ethyl Merman belting out through most of them, but it was switched to the opening number in the 1999 revival featuring Bernadette Peters.

Cody died in Denver in 1917 and is buried at 7,581 feet above sea level atop Lookout Mountain just west of the city. Even his burial was a spectacle, with 20,000 people laboring up the mountain to watch. They had to open the casket just before putting it in the ground because Mrs. Cody wanted to see the body for herself just to be sure it was really him.

The Buffalo Bill Museum and Grave is among the most popular tourist attractions in the Denver area and on any given summer day the parking lot is jammed with tour busses, RV's, and herds of motorcycles. The stuff in the museum is mostly from the *Wild West* shows— costumes, posters, and the like. One display case actually holds a pair of balls. Yes, Annie Oakley's balls! They are colored glass balls, akin to clay pigeons used as targets in marksmanship displays. They were filled with colored feathers that could easily be seen from the bleacher seats when the targets tossed into the air were smashed by bullets.

The movie in the museum at the gravesite claims that the view includes four states. That would include Wyoming, Kansas, and Nebraska, plus about 200 miles of eastern Colorado. Well, maybe on a rare, crystal clear day. But on most hazy summer days he'd be lucky to see the Coors Brewery 2,300 feet below him. Beyond that is the Mile High City and beyond that are the Great Plains, where the "buffalo" once roamed. A small herd of *Bison bison* can be seen today near the gravesite from a pullout along Interstate 70. They usually are not doing much—just standing there eating, not actually roaming. Besides being a great place to rest eternally, Buffalo Bill's Grave is also one of the best places in the Denver area for "parking" (not the kind for shopping or visiting a doctor, but the nighttime kind lovers seek for making out— doin' what comes naturally.) When the windows are not too steamed up there's no view like the Coors view. And there's no business like show business.

If you were to start at Buffalo Bill's ranch in the southwest corner of Nebraska and travel pretty much due south for five hundred miles you would find yourself in the northwest corner of Oklahoma. It is hard to think of a reason why anybody would particularly want to do particularly that without some quirky inner need to view five hundred very flat miles of grassland, but it would take you to a ranch owned by another showman of the Old West. The terrain surrounding Pawnee, Oklahoma, about an hour west of Tulsa, is flat in all directions. But the town itself sits in a surprising bit of interesting topography where Black Bear Creek meanders at the bottom of a wide valley. It was here that Gordon Lillie set up shop.

Gordon Lillie? Isn't this supposed to be about guys named Bill?

Just be patient. Here's another lad from the Midwest, this time from Illinois, who moved further west, this time to Kansas, as a teenager, and who also worked as a trapper. During his Kansas years he lived near a Pawnee Indian reservation and learned the Pawnee language. That skill became useful when he joined the crew of Buffalo Bill *Wild West Show* because he was able to act as interpreter for the Pawnees cast in the show. Somewhere in the course of his career Gordon W. Lillie was given the nickname **Pawnee Bill**. Eventually he started his own show; he called it Pawnee Bills *Historic Wild West*. It was similar to Buffalo Bill's show with the same kind of spectacle, the same shoot-'em-up and gunsmoke, the same displays of equestrian skills, the same menagerie of bison. He even had his own famous female sharpshooter—his own wife. She was an eastern gal and a Smithie (a graduate of all-female Smith College) and the daughter of a physician who was not at all happy about her going off and marrying a no-account cowboy. In the show she was billed as Champion Girls Horseback Shot of the West. The show flopped.

He made several other attempts at shows; they also flopped. However, one of his endeavors called Pawnee Bill's *Great Far East Show* was financially successful. He hired Arab jugglers and Japanese performers; the stagecoach robberies were replaced with galloping Cossacks, but Indians were still in the show. Eventually Pawnee Bill and Buffalo combined their shows into one—the *Two Bills Show*—and it lasted until movies came in. Like Buffalo Bill, Pawnee Bill also switched to making films and, like Buffalo Bill, he bought a ranch, the one in Pawnee, Oklahoma.

Pawnee, Oklahoma, is famous for three things: the 2016 earthquake, strongest ever recorded in Oklahoma; the world's largest outdoor Dick Tracy mural; and Pawnee Bill's Ranch. The ranch sits atop a rise, hardly worthy of being called a hill although the locals call it Hawk Peak with a view out over the plains and into the valley of Black Bear Creek. It has a museum filled with stuff from Native Indians and from show business—costumes, saddles, headdresses, beaded pouches and the like. There is a log cabin, a barn, and a herd of bison. The arts-and-crafts style house where Pawnee Bill and his wife lived is available for tours all year and every June the whole operation puts on a rerun of Pawnee Bill's *Original Wild West Show*. The $27.00 Deluxe Package ticket includes a reserved ring-side seat, a meal ticket, a printed program, and a bottle of water. Or you can buy a cheaper ticket but you'll have to buy a program. There's no business like show business.

Like Buffalo Bill there is no opera about him, but as for Buffalo Bill, there is a role for him in *Annie Get Your Gun*. He's doing his *Far East* show in the same town where *Buffalo Bill's Wild West* is playing. There is strife, show business-like, but it all works out in the end.

There was at least one other Midwesterner named Bill whose career resembled those of Buffalo Bill and Pawnee Bill. He is known as **Wild Bill Hickok**. He was born in Illinois and moved to Kansas. As a teenager he was too big and too tall to get a job with the Pony Express—they liked their riders skinny—so he took a job with a freight company instead. On one of his deliveries he was mauled by a bear blocking the road. Hickok survived the encounter; the bear didn't.

Besides being big, he had a protruding nose and a prominent upper lip. His early Kansas friends, one of whom was William Cody long before he became Buffalo Bill, taunted him with the nickname "Duck Bill." Like the other Bills, he worked as a scout, as a wagon master, and as an actor. But unlike the other two he served as a marshal and as a sheriff. He must have been embarrassed by the Duck Bill nickname, for once he had established himself as an important character of the West he began to call himself Wild Bill. At one point he appeared in one of Buffalo Bill's shows and at another he produced his own show—*The Daring Buffalo Chase of the Plains*. It was a flop.

He is famous mostly for two things—for his skill as a gunfighter and for getting shot himself. As a gunfighter he killed six or seven people, all bad of course, and not always as a lawman. His own murder happened during a poker game in Deadwood, South Dakota, just when it looked like he was holding a winning hand. But Jack McCall came bursting through the swinging doors of the saloon and shot him in the back of the head. The game was over.

Wild Bill was buried, and still is, in Deadwood. Beside his girlfriend Calamity Jane. The bullet that killed him was buried, and still is, in St. Louis. How that happened: The bullet that killed Hickok entered the back of his head, exited from the front, and entered the wrist of one of the other players at the table. He was another Bill—**Bill Massie**—a Mississippi River steamboat pilot. He carried the bullet around in his wrist for another thirty-four years until he died and was buried, and still is, body, bullet, and all, in Missouri.

One thing about Wild Bill Hickok that is a total fraud is his name. His official name as recorded on his birth certificate is James Butler Hickok. It also is carved into his gravestone. So from cradle to grave he was never really a Bill at all, but a Jim!

There is another noted western Bill who, based upon his name alone, was a fraud. While Buffalo Bill and Pawnee Bill are generally considered to have been white-hat good guys and Wild Bill Hickok sort of on the good guy/bad guy fence, there is little doubt that Henry McCarty was black-hat bad. In his short but highly criminal career he used several aliases, as criminals tend to do, including "Henry Antrim," "William Bonney" and "William Wright." But legend remembers him, even preserves him, as **Billy The Kid.**

He started out as a New Yorker, of all things, and moved westward as a teenager. He started wearing the traditional costume of the West—the buckskin breeches, the vest, and the sombrero. With his pink cheeks, blue eyes, yellow hair, and slim build he assimilated easily into groups of people. Folks liked him. In Kansas he fell in with a gang of disrupters and embarked upon a career of thievery, gambling, and murder. He began small, stealing clothing from a Chinese laundry. But when they locked him up as a juvie he managed to escape by shimmying up the chimney of the jail and began life as a fugitive from the law. Contrary to movie images of western outlaws, he never robbed banks, stagecoaches, nor trains. He did steal the occasional horse and rustle some odd cattle now and then but his principal crimes were simply in shooting people. He killed a fellow in Arizona (in a saloon, of course) and a blacksmith in New Mexico, then after a five-day-long fight in Lincoln, New Mexico, he became the Frontier's Most Wanted.

He was found guilty of murder in New Mexico for shooting a teenager. (Who, honestly, in the private recesses of their mind has not ever experienced a passing moment of considering doing just that?) The judge told him he was to hang until he was "dead, dead, dead" and he told the judge to go to "hell, hell, hell." While being escorted in handcuffs and shackles to the outhouse he slipped his slim wrists out of the cuffs, stole a pistol from one of his guards, and killed two of them. Eventually the sheriff caught up with him and shot him dead, dead, dead at age twenty-one.

His grave in Fort Sumner, a couple of hours east of Albuquerque, is enclosed in an iron cage to protect the stone from thieves. Consider the irony.

There is no opera about Billy The Kid but there is everything else—several novels, several plays, lots of movies and TV plots, some songs, some poems, even a ballet. The first movie was a 1911 silent flick called, simply, *Billy The Kid*. The ballet score by Aaron Copland is also called, simply, *Billy The Kid*. There was a Broadway *Billy The Kid* and a Woody Guthrie song *Billy The Kid*. **Billy Joel**—yes, another Bill—has a song *Pat Garrett and Billy The Kid*. (Pat Garrett was the sheriff who killed him.) Billy The Kid figured into the plot of TV's first episode of *Gunsmoke* in 1952. Somehow Billy The Kid has captured the romance and adventure of the Old West even more than the spectacles produced by Buffalo Bill and Pawnee Bill. Was it his gun or was it that blond hair and those blue eyes?

If the adventures and exploits of Wild Bill Hickok and Billy the Kid seem outlandish, they pale in comparison with those of another western Bill legend, that of **Pecos Bill**. This one was a genuine tough guy and a good guy at that. He was so tough that as a baby he used a bowie knife as a teething ring until he fell out of a covered wagon when his family was moving westward. The family had eighteen children so they probably did not miss the one that fell out. The fall plopped him into the Pecos River where he was swept downstream until he was rescued by a family of coyotes and raised as one of their own. Years later his brother, one of his seventeen siblings, found him and convinced him that he was not a coyote at all but indeed a human and a cowboy at that. He carried a rattlesnake named Shake that he used as a lasso and with it he once roped an entire herd of cattle all at once. Another time he lassoed a tornado and rode it like a horse. He met a gal riding down the Rio Grande on the back of a catfish and tried to impress her by shooting all of the stars out of the sky except one—the Lone Star that appears on the Texas flag. Even his death was fantastic, for he was in a saloon when a Yankee from the east came in all duded up in touristy cowboy garb—the big sombrero, the jeans, the shiny belt buckle, the chaps, and the requisite lizard skin boots, stuff you can buy in the gift shop of any truckstop in Texas—and he laughed himself to death.

But Pecos Bill was not a fraud; he just wasn't real. He was invented as a lead character in a collection of stories by one Edward O'Reilly early in the 1900's but apparently he was based upon cowboy folklore and oral tradition. One can picture a bunch of cowboys sitting around a campfire making this stuff up. As a bit of folklore (some would call it fakelore) he was highly successful, for he has appeared a variety of books, some targeted toward children and some for adults, and in several Hollywood films, including one starring Roy Rogers and another starring Patrick Swayze. There is even a restaurant named for him at Disney World.

When William Penn Adair Rogers was born the family ranch was in Indian Territory. It was in Cherokee country. Now it is in Oklahoma. You can drive there rom Pawnee Bill's Ranch in a little over an hour. Dog Iron Ranch in Oogalah, OK, is where **Will Rogers**, part Cherokee himself, roped his first steer. With nothing to do in that town, he practiced and practiced and eventually developed a repertoire of rope tricks. He could swing three lassos at once and make them all hit their target simultaneously. He could spin two of them in opposite directions around his lower legs and jump through the loops like jump-ropes without tripping. He could even do rope tricks while standing on a moving horse.

Those skills got him a job in a traveling wild west show, then at the World's Fairs of St. Louis and New York, in vaudeville, and as a headliner in the Ziegfeld Follies. But it wasn't just the rope tricks; it was also the homespun patter he performed along with it. He is often quoted; he said a lot of good things:

"I never met a man I didn't like," said Will Rogers.

"I am not a member of and organized political party. I am a Democrat," said Will Rogers.

"A fool and his money are soon elected," said Will Rogers.

"Never miss a good chance to shut up," said Will Rogers.

"Politics is the best show in the world," said Will Rogers.

"Congress—the national joke factory," said Will Rogers.

"Politics is applesauce," said Will Rogers.

"If pro is the opposite of con, what is the opposite of Congress?" asked Will Rogers.

With roles in more than seventy movies, first in silents then later in talkies, and in writing more than four thousand newspaper columns plus doing radio shows, Will Rogers, the Cowboy Philosopher, had plenty of opportunity to say lots of things. People loved him for his down to earth, genuine folksiness—not quite deadpan, but definitely low key. Long before there was *Saturday Night Live* or *Capitol Steps* he was winning over audiences with political humor. At one point he was voted most popular entertainer in Hollywood. His career ended abruptly when he was killed in a plane crash near Point Barrow, Alaska, at age fifty-five.

There is no opera about this Will either, but every once in a while he shows up as a character in a show somewhere. A Broadway musical *The Will Rogers Follies* was a biography done in Ziegfeld style with lavish feathered costumes, showgirls descending glittering stairs, spectacular rope tricks, and even one naked Indian girl. The script included many of his bits of wisdom.

There are memorials to him scattered around the United States. The Cherokee Nation runs a Will Rogers Casino and a Will Rogers Downs racetrack near Tulsa and there is a Will Rogers State Park and a Will Rogers State Beach near Hollywood. There are Will Rogers Museums in Oklahoma, California, and in Texas. Part of US 66 is designated as the Will Rogers Highway. On a mountain just outside of Colorado Springs is the Will Rogers Shrine of the Sun. On a clear day Buffalo Bill can see it from his grave on his mountain outside of Denver. But Will Rogers can't see Buffalo Bill; Will's ranch in Oklahoma is much too far away. That's where he was buried. Still is.

With mirth and laughter let old wrinkles come.
—from The Merchant of Venice, Act.I, sc.I

Avon Calling

Thousands of miles away and half a millennium later, you still cannot get away from them. Nor would you particularly want to. Those thirty-seven plays are ubiquitous, pervading into surprising areas of cultures all over the world, especially the English-speaking ones. Some people count up to thirty-eight or even thirty-nine plays, but most people settle on Thirty-Seven. The ambiguity about the correct count arises from the fact that two plays about kings named Henry come in more than one part. Should a three-part Henry count as one play or three? A two-part Henry as one or two? Regardless of the accurate total everyone would recognize this fellow as one awesomely prolific writer. By comparison, Chekhov wrote only fourteen full-length plays. Neil Simon: thirty. Tennessee Williams: twenty-four and Eugene O'Neill: thirty-one.

And the influence of those original Thirty-Seven is not limited to places that speak English. They have been translated into eighty languages, even including Klingon. Of course only dedicated Trekkies can read those. It is possible to view a performance in Arabic while sitting cross-legged on a hand-knotted oriental rug in Baghdad, in

Urdu sitting in half-lotus on a yoga mat in New Delhi, or in the Latin American version of Spanish while splayed out on a serape on the lawn of a park in Guadalajara. All the world's a stage, truly.

Seventy-three annual festivals around the globe are based on those Thirty-Seven. Even Texas has one. Of course none of them perform the entire Thirty-Seven in a single season; they generally schedule one of the tragedies, one of the comedies or histories, as well as a couple of weeks of *The Sound of Music* or *Les Miz* just to boost attendance and hope to sell subscriptions for next year. The companies associated with those festivals reach out to schools and do what George W. Bush, a Texan, would call "a heck of a job" getting youngsters interested, thus ensuring audiences for years to come. Think about it: what fourth grade boy would not be fascinated by a swordfight demo? Or three sixth grade girls by a cauldron of witch's brew? Who doesn't find something creepy about a gravedigger holding up a human skull even if it is made of plastic? Kids love this stuff. Apparently, their parents do also, for those Thirty-Seven mostly speak for themselves and manage their own audience development. They have been doing it since 1593.

The popularity is not limited to dedicated theater festivals. Just about every theater company in just about every city includes at least one of the Thirty-Seven in each season. There have been more than two hundred operas based on those plays. Ninety-seven ballets (well, okay, one of them was based on a sonnet, not a play.) And more than five hundred movies! About half of the movies were built around the plays themselves; others used the basic plots as jumping-off places—jumping off to all manner of settings and time periods.

Productions of the Thirty-Seven as have seen as many adaptations as there have been years since they originated. Take, for example, the play about Hamlet. It starts out with the young Danish prince returning home from his school's spring break in Germany to Elsinore Castle on the Danish coast. What does he find there? That his uncle has killed his father and taken up with his mother. There is no reason why Hamlet could not make his entrance in a rowboat, on a surfboard, or even in a limousine. He could arrive on a motorcycle, a tank, or a camel. He has, in fact, entered in all those ways—if you consider all the movies, all of the stagings, and all of the YouTubes ever produced. His costumes are also varied. We think of Hamlet in a black tunic and tights, but he has appeared wearing everything from gang-leather to a Speedo. Elsinore Castle has been everything from Blenheim Palace to a skyscraper.

Or take another one, the one about the star-crossed lovers from two families that don't get along. Originally, the setting was a piazza in Verona; that piazza has been played over the years by a soccer field, a high school gym, and the streets on the west side of Manhattan. The fight between the Capulets and the Montagues started out as a swordfight. The swords have been replaced with other weapons—things as deadly as guns and switchblades, and by things as lame as snowballs and Nerf balls. The Capulets and Montagues themselves have appeared in genres ranging from Mafia empires, teeny-boppers, English nobles, and street gangs.

In architecture there is a feature called the Juliet balcony. It is a small balcony, sometimes as narrow as a ledge, with a railing. They were all the rage in Verona. In the original script of the play there is no mention of a balcony at all—she appears "above" in a window. Somehow over the years that scene has become known as "the balcony scene" and in modern theatrical adaptations, that balcony has been played—again considering all possible permutations ever produced—by things as varied as stepladders, pedestals, fire escapes, and even hot tubs. In the original play Romeo doesn't ascend to the window, he merely "exits." But many directors find it more romantic for him to go up there and he has climbed up a grapevine, ascended on a trapeze, a forklift, an elevator, and, of course, lots of steps and ladders. Juliet herself has been seen wearing Renaissance garb, 1920's flapper skirts, Christian Dior, Eddie Bauer, Victoria's Secret, and sometimes wearing nothing at all.

Juliet Capulet
couldn't stay abstinent
once her beau Romeo
from rival House Montague
arranged for a rendezvous
out on her parapet.

He thought he would try for
one last kiss to die for.
He climbed up to meet her;
what could be sweeter.

They found themselves soon
in the gloom of a room
of a Veronese tomb
doomed to presume,
but who poisoned whom?

The plays have been adapted to animation, to puppetry, to various forms of dance, and even—on the theory that actions speak louder than words—to mime. But one of the most intriguing adaptations was done by a group of students at Exeter University. That's only two hours from Stratford on the M5 but it could not be further "out." They staged thirty-five of the plays using household objects as characters. Juliet was a jar of marmalade; Hamlet was a bottle of vinegar. (Talk about sweet and sour!). Other roles were played by balls of twine, by paper cups, by empty beer mugs, by pretty much whatever. The surprising thing is that it works. They have been doing it for more than thirty years and have even exported a company to New York.

New York itself made national news in 2017 when a free production of *Julius Caesar* in Central Park featured an actor in the title role costumed with a red necktie and turmeric-yellow coif to look like Donald Trump. Just after the violent stabbing scene the performance came to a halt when two activists—obviously pro-Tumpers—jumped onto the stage and raised loud vocal protestations of violence against the Donald. Once the security folks got them taken away the play resumed with what happened to be the next line of the script, "Liberty! Freedom!" The audience rose in enthusiastic applause.

To the best of our knowledge, the author of those Thirty-Seven never visited New York, or anywhere else America, for that matter. But all over America there are cities and towns whose names derive from his titles or characters. There are Othellos in New Jersey, North Carolina, and Washington. Romeos in Colorado, Michigan, Tennessee, and Florida. The population of all those Romeos put together adds up to only 4,604, but throw in Romeoville, Illinois, and it goes up to 40,000. The reason the one in Illinois is big enough to skew the total is that it is possible to commute from there to a job in Chicago. The other Romeos are pretty much in the boonies. Hamlet really gets around; there are Hamlets in North Dakota, Nebraska, Illinois, North Carolina, New York, Indiana, and Ohio. Ophelia, Hamlet's girlfriend, is in Virginia and Oklahoma. Cleopatra and Brutus are in Kentucky; Caesar is in Mississippi.

Not to be outdone by all this, even Texas gets into it. At the very top of the state, in the Panhandle region, is a Stratford. South of that, and of course pretty much everything in Texas is south of that, are towns called Iago, Desdemona, and Viola. There is also Texas Olivia and a Texas Paris. They also have their own Caesar; after all, somebody has to be responsible for the salad. Not that it matters, but the Caesar in Mississippi with a population of 10,878, is five times bigger than the one in Texas.

A dream of every middle-class American parent is to take the kids to Orlando to visit Disney World for spring break. In fact, many view it as a requirement, a family rite of passage. But once there, after paying the mega-fee for admission, the family dream begins to fall apart. The lines are long, there is urgent need for a bathroom but they don't want to lose their position in the line. Family squabbles develop. Somebody is hungry. Somebody is tired. Somebody is hot. Somebody gets bratty. It probably would not help much, but Daddy could try a diversionary tactic of explaining to the fussy kid how special it is to be in Orlando, how lucky they are to be there with the palm trees, the alligators, and the warm weather. Try talking about Orlando, the character. Try explaining how Orlando is probably the second-most famous lover out of the

Thirty-Seven and how he wooed his beloved Rosalind by nailing love poems to the trees in the Arden forest. Sure. Just go ahead and try that.

If the kid is still bratty and all he wants to do is to get on the Space Mountain ride and doesn't give a singular solitary twit about Orlando and Rosalind there is still a last resort to stop the fussing: threaten to take him to the Orlando in Oklahoma. Population 148; he will love it. No lines.

Names like those are not limited to this planet. Uranus, the seventh planet out from the sun and a very long way from Stratford Upon Avon, has twenty-seven moons. Twenty-five of them are named for characters from the Thirty-Seven. The two biggest ones were discovered in 1787 by a Bill—one **William Herschel**—who called them simply "Number One" and "Number Two." His son, probably thinking that sounded too much like potty talk, named them Titania and Oberon. Two more were discovered in 1858 by yet another Bill—**William Lassel**—who named Ariel and Umbriel. Most of the others were not discovered until NASA's *Voyager 2* did a flyby in the 1980's. The NASA folks continued the tradition of nomenclature and now we have, orbiting around Uranus as it orbits around the sun that we share, a prolific *dramatis personae* that includes most of the big names from the Thirty-Seven. Like Desdemona, Ophelia, Cordelia, and, of course, Juliet. Neither Romeo or Hamlet made the cut, at least so far. Telescopes keep getting better; flybys get closer. There may be hope for Hamlet yet.

Cordelia, Ophelia, and Emilia
each endured strife
from a man in her life.

The first had trouble with her dad
out on the heath decidedly mad.
The second's problem was her lover
and she drowned before the play was over.
The third one was Iago's wife;
her husband stabbed her with a knife.

The lesson from these tales of woe
as these three ladies tell us so:
    The way to survive
    and still be alive
    at the end of Act V
    is to steer wide and clear
    of fellows like Lear
    or Princes of Denmark
    or cads like Iago.

    It's best to forgo
    all sense of ego
    and simply go
        solo.

You don't need to go to Uranus to experience the present-day influence of those nearly five-hundred-year-old plays. You don't even need to go to the theater. Beside the Bayshore Freeway near the San Francisco Airport there was a billboard advertising a popular brand of potato chips. It showed two fourteen-foot high figures in togas, one Caesar-like with a laurel crown and the other Brutus-like with a lean and hungry look. The Caesarish one, holding the bag of chips with the brand name boldly displayed, has reached in and is offering a chip to the Brutus-looking one. The caption: *"Et one, Brute?"* You don't need to know much about Renaissance theater to recognize immediately where that one came from.

There is also a problem that arises when booking an airline ticket, at least when it comes to choosing a seat if you are lucky enough to find an airline that allows doing that. Sometimes they charge you extra for a seat assignment, but sometimes it is worth it. Suppose you are viewing the seat map and see that the middle seat of the second row is available. Trouble is, that's a middle seat and you don't want to share armrests with two strangers all the way from Newark to Phoenix. There are some aisle seats way in the back; but by the time you get back there the overhead luggage bins might be full. So, a decision. A question: 2b or not?

Outside of St. Louis there is a breakfast joint that serves a ham omelet called the Hamlet. The fellow back in the kitchen manning the griddle? His name is Larry, a.k.a. Fryer Laurence.

In recent years the second most common name given to baby girls is Olivia, like the comedic and romantic hero of *Twelfth Night*; it is more

53

popular among girls than Will is in boys. Juliet ranks number 226, Ophelia 580. (The answer to what you are questioning: #1 is Emma.)

> Rosalind's red.
> Viola's blue.
> Bianca can't wed
> because her sister's a shrew.

> Cleopatra, Queen of Denial,
> weighed Tony's offer a long, long while.
> Although it would wed her to power in Rome
> It would take her away from her New Kingdom Home.
> Finally, finding it too harsh and too heinous,
> She said he could shove it up his Coriolanus.

Whether all of this is as you like it or whether it is what you will, you really can't get away from them.

A baby hamster is called a hamlet.

Hecate's Brew

Nutrition Facts

Serving size: **1 half-litre**

Servings per cauldron: **about 50**

100% organic. **100% gluten-free**

Contains no antibiotics. No GMO
No added MSG.
Calories per serving: 150

Total fat 50g (40%Daily Value), Saturated fat 10g (10%DV), Cholesterol 50mg(50%DV), Sodium 410mg (18%DV) Total Carbohydrate 210g (80%DV) Dietary fiber 1g (4%DV) Total sugars 30g (20%DV) Protein 7g (13%DV) Bone tissue 400mg(20%DV)

Ingredients: fillet of fenny snake, eye of newt, toe of frog, Adder's fork, blind-worm's sting, lizard leg, owlet's wing, scale of dragon, root of hemlock, gall of goat, slips of yew, non-specified poisoned entrails. May also contain traces of Tartar's lips, nose of Turk, or finger of birth-strangled babe.

WARNING: Processed in a facility that uses baboon blood for cooling.

Best prepared over open fire and served bubbling hot. Most effective charm obtained if served in thunder, lightning, or in rain.

Use Before: Birnam Wood to Dunsinane shall come.

What the American public wants is a tragedy with a happy ending.
—William Dean Howells

PlayBills

Many Bills have earned top billing in the varied world of entertainment. In theater you will find them onstage, backstage, in the orchestra pit, and in management. While you are waiting for the curtain to go up you can pass the time by studying the copy of *Playbill* that your usher gave you. Look at all of those names in the back—the lighting designers, the understudies, the choreographers. There are bound to be some Bills listed in there somewhere. The same goes for Bills in movies and TV. Take a good look as the credits roll by and there will be Bills listed as Cinematographers, Costume Designers, and Film Editors. You probably have a somewhat accurate idea what kind of work those fellows do, but you may not have any earthly idea what some of the others do, like the Key Grip, the Gaffer, and the Best Boy, but some of them are likely to be Bills and apparently nobody can make a movie without them.

Stage Bills

One of America's best-loved and most enduring musicals is *Carousel*, a mid-twentieth century show with music by Richard Rodgers and lyrics by Oscar Hammerstein. The central character is **Billy Bigelow**, a carnival barker who operates a merry-go-round. When the traveling carnival has a gig at a small New England coastal town he falls in love with a local millworker named Julie. He knocks her up. In a moving soliloquy he sings about how wonderful it will be to have a son. He will, of course, name him Bill—the perfect name for Number One Son." He, "my boy Bill" will grow to be tall and strong like his father. Son Bill will be free to become whatever he wants; he can be a champion prizefighter, he'll be tough, nothing sissy about him—thoroughly butch. He could even be President. They will go fishing together, they will wrestle, they will be pals. It will be great to be a father to Bill. But then he realizes— oh, no, Bill, how *could* you? What if—no, you wouldn't dare. You're not even born yet, what if you turned out to be, you *traitor*, of all things, a *girl*!

All of that happens in Act 1. Then in Act 2 things turn dark. Billy, the father, desperate to support his wife Julie and the forthcoming baby, becomes involved in a robbery and gambling scheme that turns bad. He commits suicide before the baby is born. In a contrived plot twist, he can revisit his family after his death and sometimes they can see him but sometimes he is invisible. Sounds corny, but it works. In the very last scene of the play or the movie he looks in on his child's high school graduation. The child's name, by the way, is Louise.

An even more depressing Bill in American theater is **Willy Loman**, the central character of Arthur Miller's *Death of a Salesman*. The play, about two hours long, is about the last twenty-four hours of a worn-out, frustrated dreamer defeated by the capitalist system. He commits suicide at the end of Act 2. For a play that is such a downer, it has had surprising success. It has been performed on stages all over America since its 1949 Broadway opening and every once in while it is even revived there. There is a movie, of course, but, at least so far, no musical or ice extravaganza versions. All that could change, though, if someone comes along with enough dark creativity and enough money. Look, they did a musical about Eva Peron, of all subjects, and it worked. Same with Alexander Hamilton; that one sort of worked too. Perhaps there is hope for Willy.

Both *Salesman* and *Carousel* started out as stage plays and became movies later. One Billy, though, did it the other way around. ***Billy Elliot*** hit the big screen first. The story is about an eleven-year-old kid in the Midlands of England—coal mining country—in the middle of the 1980's. Not only was there a miners' strike going on and a very conservative Margaret Thatcher doing her best to close the mines, but Billy, in this macho tough guy mining environment, wanted to be, of all things, a ballet dancer. It has a feel-good ending; he becomes a principal *danseur* at the Royal Ballet. The 2000 movie was an enormous success. Successful enough to spawn a West End musical version, called—just so there would be absolutely no confusion about it—*Billy Elliot the Musical*. (It is a musical.) Elton John wrote the music (for the musical.) Opening in 2005, it was wildly successful in London but it was thought to be too Britain-specific to take to Broadway. However, a New York production of *Billy Elliot the Musical* (the musical version) opened in 2008. It won ten Tony awards and ran for four years. One of its awards, since it was a *musical*, was for Best Musical.

Believe it or not, there was a staged version musical of Herman Mellville's *Moby Dick*, called *Moby Dick! The Musical.* The plot differs widely from the Mellville story. This one, staged in England, was about a private school for young ladies that, finding itself in desperate financial difficulty (they were going broke), decided to raise funds by staging a performance of *Moby Dick* in their swimming pool. The headmistress was played in drag by the same actor who played Captain Ahab. It was a whale of a tale. Herman Mellville's *other* seagoing book, **Billy Budd**, had had more success on stages than did poor *Moby*. After all, this one did not require a whale. The story is about a handsome, likeable young sailor accused of mutiny and tried for murder—hardly the stuff of crowd-pleaser theater. There have been at least three movie versions, all of them successful, several TV adaptations, and at least one Broadway musical. The latter was not called *Billy Budd The Musical*, but simply *Billy*. It closed after a single performance in 1969. A straight drama version, *Billy Budd*, had fared a little better about a decade earlier. That one ran for 105 performances. There are two opera versions. The score for better-known, more frequently produced one is by Benjamin Britten and its libretto—in English—is by E.M. Forster. The opera premiered at Covent Garden in the same year that the drama version opened in America. The opera, though, is still around. Just about every major opera company in the world, including the Metropolitan, revives it every few years. The title role is a plum prize for a young performer with good looks and a strong baritone voice.

Another opera, ***Willie Stark***, is less known. Based on Robert Penn Warren's novel *All the King's Men*, it tells the dark story of a corrupt Louisiana governor's struggles to avoid impeachment. He does manage to do that; he is assassinated instead.

Screen Bills

One of the most influential Willies in American culture never experienced what is his now-expected fifteen minutes of fame. ***Steamboat Willie*** was a riverboat in a 1928 movie with the same name, back when "talkies" were still a novelty. The movie about it lasts only eight minutes. Produced in black and white, it was one of the first animated cartoons with a synchronized sound track. Few people remember much about the movie itself, but two things about it have lasting significance: its star and its producer. The star was Mickey Mouse. The producer was Walt Disney. Mickey Mouse is still around; Walt, who also voiced what little dialogue there was in the film, is not, although there is an unsubstantiated rumor that his body is frozen in a vat of liquid nitrogen somewhere awaiting revival by thawing at some point in the future. Thanks to the success of *Steamboat Willie* about a century ago, The Walt Disney Company is ubiquitous—still producing blockbuster films and running a vast entertainment empire that now includes Broadway shows, a cable TV network, and theme parks and resorts on both coasts of America as well as in Tokyo, Paris, and Hong Kong.

Following the success of *Steamboat Willie* and Mickey Mouse, a few years later another popular cartoon character had a movie debut—*Popeye The Sailor*. The movie included a very tame version of an old drinking song **Barnacle Bill the Sailor**. Movies didn't have MPAA ratings back in 1933, but if they did, this one would have been rated **G**. Anybody, kids included, could watch it. Barroom versions of that song, though, would be labeled **X**. The song, in its seminal barroom version, was originally called Bollocky Bill, but that title was deemed too raunchy, too suggestive, too *testicular*, for public consumption in situations where vast amounts of beer were not involved. The Popeye movie was targeted toward families, not to pub crawlers, so they replaced the word "bollocky" with "barnacle"—equally alliterative with "Bill" and equally dactylic for the rhythm of the song. It also carried the bonus of being sailor-related. In the beered-up versions, whoever can come up with the raunchiest lyrics wins a free round. As with many limericks, the most effective verses—the ones that earn the boldest **X**'s and the loudest hurrahs—involve frequent use of slang terms for gender-specific body parts and things that can be done with them to other people's body parts, as well as suggestive rhymes built on place names like Bangkok or Nantucket. You can find some good ones on YouTube. But use **PG**, parental guidance, if there are children present.

Another Bill movie, an old one, is about as **G** as a film can get—*Bill and Coo*. It was filmed just after World War II and, if nothing else, offered welcome relief from years of tension. The plot, not very original, has all of the elements of classic melodrama—the damsel in distress (Coo), the villain, and the hero (Bill). What was different about this one was the cast: not Hollywood celebrities, but live birds. Yes, real birds. In people costumes. Bill and Coo, the lovebirds of the title, were played by actual lovebirds. The villain was a crow. The whole thing was apparently just *aww, darling.*

A movie at the extreme other end of the cutesy-to-violent spectrum is *Kill Bill.* There are actually two movies, filmed a couple of years apart, *Kill Bill Vol. I* and *Kill Bill Vol. II.* They are rated **R** for including "bloody violence, sexual content" and "language" throughout. It would be difficult to make a film about assassins and revenge without any violence and it would be even more difficult to sell it these days if it did not contain "language." Each of those films runs about two hours, but there is a third version, *Kill Bill: The Whole Bloody Affair,* that combines both "volumes" and runs a tad longer than four hours. It must be very good, for the online film info site IMDB gives it a rating of 8.8; that's about as high as any movie ever gets. Trouble is, hardly anybody has seen it because it has been shown only at a few film festivals with restricted admission and has never been released for home viewing in any form. But it's a good thing that it's good, because otherwise four hours would be a long sit.

Quite a few movies have Bills in their cast or involved in the production; some of them—the actors, directors, and producers are listed here later in the Birthdays chapter. A few films have Bill in their title. One of them *Bill & Ted's Excellent Adventure* was successful enough to spawn at least two offspring: *Bill & Ted Face the Music* and

Bill & Ted's Bogus Journey. The first one was the best. Two high school kids, about to flunk their history class, get involved in a time travel adventure that allows them to interact with the likes of Joan of Arc, Beethoven, Genghis Khan, and Napoleon. There is even a documentary about the Bill & Ted franchise called *Bill & Ted Go To Hell*. Curiously, that one had the highest rating of them all.

One Bill movie is called just that—*Bill*. Nothing beyond that, just *Bill*. It is about a mentally disabled Bill who was institutionalized until he was taken in by a kind family and eventually found love. It starred Mickey Rooney. Sorry.

The title of the film *Bill W.* implies somebody more specific, yet allows a bit of mystery about who the *W* stands for; it somehow implies anonymity. That is thoroughly appropriate, for the film is a documentary biography of **William Griffith Wilson**, who co-founded Alcoholics Anonymous, often referred to simply as "AA," in 1935. The goal of AA was to help members recover from lives of alcohol-induced despair into lives of hope and control. Current membership globally is approximately two million. Members of AA call themselves "friends of Bill" and there are more than 60,000 "meetings" groups in the US alone. That is enough so that there is a chapter close to pretty much anybody who needs one. They occur even on cruise ships, where the daily calendar of activities included a five o'clock meeting for Friends of Bill. So when it's five o'clock somewhere there is a safe respite for those who need support. The movie describes Bill W.'s own struggles, his own recovery, and the establishment of the Twelve Step program that is helping millions.

Probably one of the most misleading titles ever put on the screen was *Wild Bill*, for anyone reading that title would immediately assume it is a film about Wild Bill Hickock. But no, it isn't. It isn't even a western. It tells the story of a Bill released on parole back into working-class London who finds that his wife has abandoned their two teen-aged sons and has left them to fend for themselves. That's a lot of challenge for a fresh parolee to deal with, but he does. He must. It is a moving drama.

One of the hit family movies in the last decade of the last century was *Free Willy*. It was successful enough to spawn two sequels, called *Free Willy 2* and *Free Willy 3*. The character of Willy in all them was played by a whale, for the Willy series follows the story of an Oregon kid who bonds with an orca doomed to a boring life of swimming circular laps in a fish tank at an aquarium. Considering the title of the film, it is not surprising that said kid succeeds in getting said whale to jump out of said tank and back into the ocean where he belongs. But troubles lurk in the open Pacific, so in Willy 2 he is rescued from and oil spill and in Willy 3 he is saved from an illegal whaler who would convert him to sushi. The same whale played Willy in all three films. His name was Keiko. He lived twenty-seven years until he died of pneumonia in the chilly waters of a Norwegian fjord.

There is no way that actor Matt Damon could ever be considered as a William. We know him as Jason Bourne, the chap with the identity and the ultimatum, as Mr. Ripley, the talented one, and as Private Ryan, the WWII paratrooper who was saved. But in his breakout role, the one that made him a Hollywood favorite, he played a Will—in *Good*

Will Hunting. In that role he played a janitor with an uncanny gift for mathematics. Although we are only supposed to be considering first name Williams, not last name Williams, in these pages, it is relevant, especially since he won an Oscar for it, that that actor who played the psychiatrist that put Will on good footing was a Williams, Robin Williams.

If you are looking for Bills, Williams, and Wills among Oscar winners, there is not very good Will hunting there. In fact, it is pretty piss-poor. Of the 70-odd males who have won the Academy Award for Best Performance by an Actor in a Leading Role and the 60-odd who have won the award for Best Performance by an Actor in a Supporting Role (commonly referred to as the Oscars for "best actor "and for "best supporting actor") only one of them was a Bill. That was **William Hurt**, who took home the statuette in 1985 for his role as a gay man in a South American prison in *Kiss of the Spider Woman.*

Song Bills

Just as Bills have found their way into subjects and titles of movies, they also have made significant inroads into popular music.

Anyone in America who is old enough for an AARP discount probably remembers a song that topped the charts for weeks in the late 1960's and prompted water-cooler discussions about what exactly was going on in the song *Ode to Billy Joe.* The lyrics are enigmatic. **Billy Joe MacAllister** has jumped off the Tallahatchie Bridge in Mississippi.

The question is: Why? A year earlier, according to the local gossip mill, Billy Joe and his girlfriend had been seen on the bridge throwing something overboard. Something, but what? That's where the mystery lay. Was it a ring? Flowers, maybe? Or even a baby? The thing is—and this was the point of the song—that to the folks in the little Mississippi town, it doesn't matter what it was. It doesn't even matter that Billy Joe eventually threw himself over the railing. Big deal. Life goes on; pass the biscuits please.

An even older Bill-based song, also set in Mississippi, is *Won't You Come Home, Bill Bailey*. This one is still around as a jazz classic, ragtime and Dixieland favorite. The lyrics are about a young woman who is married to a philandering husband, a timeless story. **Bill Bailey** really existed. He was an entertainer in the saloons of Jackson, a railroad town at the time, filled every evening with roughnecks, roustabouts and gandy dancers who had been working on the railroad all the live-long day. His wife got fed up with his constant carousing, kicked him out, and later regretted it. He told one his buddies about it one night in a saloon. The buddy was a songwriter and the rest, as they say, is history.

Those same senior discount folks also recall singer Peggy Lee, famous for her versions of *Fever* and *Is That All There is?* Included in her seven-decades-long career were several Bill songs, two of which made the charts. One of them, ***Big Bad Bill***, tells of a once tough fellow, a fighting man. Then he found himself a wife and changed his ways. He's sweet William now. The other hit was simply called ***Bill.*** No adjectives, Just *Bill*, like the *Bill* movie mentioned above. *Bill*, that is all there is.

This Bill, described in only eight lines of lyrics, is mild-mannered, unheroic, even forgettable. But she loves him; he's just her Bill.

Since the name Bill in any of its forms—like William, Willy, and all of the other variations—is so common, it is not at all surprising to find dozens of them sprinkled throughout lists of A-list entertainers. (**Bill Pullman**, **William Shatner**, **Billy Ray Cyrus**) One Bill deserves special mention—**Bill Robinson**. Chances are, you have never heard of Bill Robinson. But you have probably heard of his nickname "Bojangles." He was a dancer, an actor, and a singer. But mostly a dancer. Yes, he'd dance for you. In worn-out shoes. But not in blackface; he didn't need that.

He was born in Virginia in 1878, a place and a time very difficult to be Black in, but once he established himself on stage, he entertained both Black and white audiences alike. His career as a tap dancer took him into many forms of entertainment, enough that an outline of his career reads like a synopsis of entertainment history. To wit:

minstrel → vaudeville → Broadway → Hollywood → television
1900's   1910's   1920's   1930's   1940's

A recent internet posting lists the twenty highest-paid Blacks in the world. Seventeen of them are entertainers or sports figures. It was no different in Bill Robinson's "Bojangles" day, except that Blacks were not as prominent in sports then as they are now. He was always in great demand and was the highest paid Black entertainer of his day. Near the end of his career, his fame enabled him to call attention to civil rights issues and he was somewhat of a philanthropist. When he died in 1949, too soon to witness the progress in civil rights that began about twenty years later and too soon for color TV, IMAX, Netflix, and YouTube, schools in Harlem were closed so that children and their families could listen to the radio broadcast of his funeral. In 1989 a joint U.S. House/Senate resolution designated his birthday, May 25, as National Tap Dance Day. He is gone, but tap dancing, the medium that he took to new levels, goes on.

Shortly after the middle of 1900's there were the Beatles who brought a new style of music from across the pond. Before the Beatles there was Elvis, yes, Elvis the Pelvis, whose musical style and pubic choreography combined folk, rock, and sex. Everyone knew his latest recording. And before Elvis there was **Bill Haley**. He and his band, Bill Haley and The Comets, are the ones who can be credited with establishing the Rock and Roll genre into America forever. Their hit songs—*Shake, Rattle, and Roll* and *Rock Around the Clock*—are still heard on Oldies but Goodies stations today.

Cable Bills

A 2017 British TV series, entitled simply as *Will*, was about England's most famous Will—the one from Stratford Upon Avon. The show was about his arrival in London and his struggles to get a theatre going there. It was more soap opera than history and it ran for 10 episodes.

That pales in comparison to *The Bill Cosby Show*, the American comedy series that ran for 197 episodes. In this one, **Bill Cosby** played the role of Dr. Cliff Huxtable, a Black pediatrician with a lawyer wife.

The show and its actors were much-loved. He was known as "America's Dad." From his early days as a stand-up comedian through his stardom in films and TV, Cosby himself entertained audiences for six decades. Then everything fell apart in 2018 when he was convicted of sexual assault and sent to prison. He was released three years later on a legal technicality, but the damage was done. His reputation was shot.

But that Most Episodes Ever to a TV Will-Show Award, if there were such a thing, goes to *Will and Grace*. 246 episodes! That's about three times more than *The Sopranos*. The setup for *Will and Grace* had a gay lawyer sharing a flat with a straight interior designer—a woman. It was successful because it was funny, but it also had significance as one of the first shows not embarrassed by gayness.

When it comes to longevity in the public eye, few can exceed that of *Star Trek*'s **William Shatner**. Canadian-born, his acting career began in Shakespearian mode at the Stratford Shakespeare Festival in Stratford, Ontario. Then followed some American TV roles that did not generate widespread excitement until his big—*really* big—role as Captain Kirk, commander of the U.S.S Enterprise in the original *Star Trek* series nearly sixty years ago. The mission of the enterprise crew was to boldly go where no man has gone before. They pursed that mission—split infinitive be damned—spawning the first generation of enthusiastic Trekkies, for 79 episodes in three seasons before it was cancelled. In almost every episode Shatner's character had a different love interest, the most memorable one occurring in a November, 1968 episode when he participated in the very first interracial kiss on scripted television. Shatner's involvement with *Star Trek* pretty much ended with the cancellation of the series, but *Star Trek* itself is still very much with us, for there have been a dozen *Star Wars* films, at least six of them box office blockbusters. The current generation of Trekkies is probably even more enthusiastic than the first, with sales of toy light sabers, Darth Vader masks, and Trekkie costumes soaring, especially near Halloween. An annual convention, held in a different American city each year, attracts 15,000 attendees. Many of them boldly go appropriately costumed. So if you find yourself seated in a plane beside Darth Vader on a flight to Las Vegas you know what he's up to. May the Force be with him.

As for recognition, Bills have done better in television than in the movies. The Will hunting is better there, for while only one Bill has won a Best Actor Oscar, eight have won Emmys. One of them, **Bill Cosby**, won them in two categories—Leading Actor in a Comedy Series and Outstanding Lead Actor in a Drama Series (*The Bill Cosby Show* and *I Spy.)* **William Daniels** won four years in a row starting in 1983 for his role in *St. Elsewhere* and **William Macy** won five times for *Shameless,* the earliest in 2014. The other five were William Windon (*My World and Welcome to It,)* **Bill Bixby** (*The Courtship of Eddie's Father,)* **Will Forte** (*The Last Man on Earth,)* **William Conrad** (*Cannon,)* and **Billy Porter** (*Pose.)* If you have never heard of some of them or the shows they were in you either don't watch the right channels or you are two generations too young. Just as baby boys are less frequently named William these days, recent Emmy winners tend to have more trendy names like Jason, Kit and Kevin. And Brian with an *i*. That happens in the Oscars too; recent winners have more Gen X names like Joaquin, Rami, Casey, and Colin.

The Oscars, everybody has heard of them. Why are they Oscars, not Oswalds, Owens, Olivers, or somebody elses? Because when the lady who was Director of Academy of Motion Picture Arts and Sciences (the "Academy") first saw the statue in 1931 she thought it looked like her uncle Oscar. Apparently, she was accustomed to seeing her uncle freshly waxed and shiny, totally naked, but not very anatomically correct. He is missing some critical parts. The Tony Awards are not as widely known as the Oscars, but in Broadway circles they are just as coveted. Their name derives from Antoinette Perry, an actress, producer and theatre director who was co-founder and secretary of the American Theatre Wing, the organization that grants the awards. Her BFF's called her "Tony."

Television's Emmy Awards are not named for anybody at all; the name is a personified version of "immie," which is a nickname for a type of camera—an image orthicon tube—used in the earliest days of television. The derivation of the name for the Grammy Awards, for music, is more obvious. They are not named for anybody's grandmother, but for an early type of record player called a gramophone—one of those contraptions with a needle that courses through a continuous groove picking up vibrations from a spinning disk and emits sound through a brass bell that looks somewhat like a French horn. The award statuette is a mini version of one.

To win all four awards, an Emmy, a Grammy, an Oscar, and a Tony, is to win the grand slam of entertainment. You are an EGOT winner. Only sixteen people have accomplished that (none of them are Bills.) It is tough enough to score wins in all four EGOT prizes, even tougher to add a win in a fifth category that would make you a BEGOT winner.

BEGOT? Tucked into the hills way up in the northeast corner of Georgia, closer to Chatanooga than to Atlanta, is the city of Dalton. And tucked into the middle of Dalton is a community theatre, the Dalton Little Theatre. Like many community theatres across America, DLT is run totally by volunteers—volunteer actors, volunteer directors, volunteer stage hands, volunteer ushers, volunteer everythings. And every one of them is wildly enthusiastic about their role. The organization has been in operation since 1869. It nearly dissolved just after WWII and the theatre came close to going dark forever, but it was rescued by a mover/shaker named **William B. Davies** who infused enough energy and skills to keep the lights on. DLT is currently housed in an abandoned firehouse, and once a year everybody gets together for an evening presentation of their own William B. Davies Awards, the "Billy Awards." So to be a BEGOT winner you would need to do some time in Georgia before moving on to Hollywood or the Great White Way. The Billy Awards, like ones in the more widely-known EGOT realm, are given in familiar categories like Best Actor, Best Actress, and the like, but the Billy Awards include one category that the pros certainly will never include: Best Volunteer. The reason? Volunteers don't get paid.

We are imperfect. We cannot expect perfect government.
—William Howard Taft

Capitol Hill Billies

In the roughly two and a quarter centuries since the United States of America has existed as a constitutional entity we have had presidents named Bill for about ten percent of the time. It has taken four different fellows—rich, white guys named William—to achieve that.

We have also had two Vice President Bills, but since neither of them ascended to the presidency they never became household names. One of them, **William A. Wheeler**, who was Veep under Rutherford B. Hayes, served one four-year term stating in 1877. Unlike most politicians then and now, he somehow managed to gain a reputation for honesty. His refusal to accept a pay raise probably had something to do with that.

The other V.P. named Bill was Alabama's **William Rufus DeVane King**, who held the office only 45 days beginning in March of 1853 and never really served at all. Suffering from tuberculosis, he had gone to Cuba for his health, thinking that some warm, humid Caribbean air would be more beneficial to his lungs than the unsettled March air of Alabama or Washington. Congress passed special legislation that allowed him to take the oath of office in the foreign country. Realizing that his health was not improving, he returned to his Alabama home where he died the day after his arrival. There's no place like home. The office of Vice President was vacant for the next four years.

Illness also shortened the service time for one of our President Bills—**William Henry Harrison**. He did not contribute much to our total Bill-time because he caught a cold while delivering a two-hour inaugural address in Washington, D.C. in early March, three weeks before the hardiest cherry blossoms even began to think about Spring, without wearing a hat or a coat. He attended a round of inaugural parties in a wet shirt and his cold progressed into pneumonia. At least that was the popular rumor at the time and one that persisted for about another 180 years. Recent evidence, though, suggests that his death might have been due to typhoid fever caused by bacteria in the White House water supply. Apparently, it was contaminated by drainage from a nearby marsh. They should have drained the swamp. His doctors treated him with the most effective remedies available at the time— bloodletting, suction cups, and live snakes. He died one month later in Indianapolis, Indiana, of all places, before his wife had even moved to the White House to measure the windows for drapery. He, William Henry Harrison, our ninth president, is not to be confused with the other President Harrison who was his own grandson Benjamin and our twenty-third president.

Grandpa William's nickname was "Old Tippecanoe". He earned that moniker while he was Governor of Indiana Territory by leading

U.S. forces against a strong Shawnee chief named Tecumseh in a battle along an otherwise peaceful riverbank in Indiana at a place called Tippecanoe, whose name derives from a native word meaning "buffalo fish place." It doesn't make a whole lot of sense, but that is what it means. For twenty-one years starting in 1799 he was a member of the Democratic-Republican Party before switching to the Whigs. Obviously, he covered all the bases. And quite successfully. At the time he became president at age 68 he was the oldest man to do so. People had another nickname for him: "Old Granny." This, of course, was well before Reagan, Trump, and Biden, who were well into their 70's when they took the oath.

Nearly sixty years later we got another President William, an Ohio Republican named McKinley, **William McKinley**, our 25th President. The election of 1896 was a hotly contested one, pitting two Williams against each other. The rival was a Nebraska Democrat named William Jennings Bryan. Bryan-with-a-*y* had advantage and reputation as an accomplished orator and could enthrall audiences gathered to hear him orate from flag-draped cabooses at railroad whistlestops across the nation. He wanted American currency to be based on silver. McKinley preferred gold. It may seem odd to us today to think that a major issue in a campaign would be the chemistry of metals, but that was indeed the case. Most of the major newspapers of the day supported Bryan. An exception was the New York Journal headed by yet another William— **William Randolph Hearst**. Gold won. McKinley was inaugurated in March of 1897.

He had lots of nicknames, some based on his Buckeye State origins: "Ohio Napoleon," and "The Idol of Ohio." Some based on lifestyle; "Rough and Ready," "The Cowboy," and "The Lion." And some based on who-knows-what, like "Wobbly Willie" and "The Human Iceberg."

His first term was successful enough to win him election to a second. But six months into it, while climbing a set of steps up to the Temple of Music at the Pan-American Exposition in Buffalo, New York, he was assassinated. He took two bullets in the torso. His doctor could get only one out. Despite considerable probing and poking the doctor simply could not find the other one. Part of the problem might have been that the doctor was a gynecologist and therefore unaccustomed to probing into regions of the body that high up. Gangrene developed; McKinley died.

Shortly after McKinley's death lots of things were named after him—schools, parks, streets and such. Even a mountain in Alaska. The way that happened was that a gold prospector in Alaska, upon learning that McKinley—the gold standard guy—had just won the election, started calling it Mount McKinley to celebrate the gold victory. A quarter of a century later the U.S. government made the name official when it established Mount McKinley National Park. There had always been some grumbling about it among the native populations of the region who had previously referred to it as Denali, which in the native tongue means "the great one." The native meaning of this one, unlike that of Tippecanoe, actually makes sense, for not only is the mountain spectacularly beautiful but it is also distinguished as the highest peak on the continent of North America. At 20,310 feet, it is indeed "great."

The name persisted; the grumbling also. Every time there was any sort of proposal to change the name back to Denali it met with objection from Ohioans. The mountain, in their view, should be named for their guy even though it is four thousand miles away. The Eskimos claimed that they named it first. The matter festered for decades until 2015 when President Barack Obama, a Democrat, took action by executive order and declared the mountain Denali. So the Eskimos won. Ohio's electoral votes had been cast for Obama in both the 2008 and 2012 elections but in 2016, the first election since renaming the great mountain, those Ohio votes went for the Republican candidate. Obviously, the Ohioans were pissed.

A curious legacy of the President McKinley phenomenon is the choice of Ohio's state flower, the red carnation. It is indeed a strange choice considering that carnations will not grow in Ohio, at least not all year round outdoors. But apparently more obvious choices were rejected. The dogwood blossom, prolific in Ohio springtimes, was already selected by several other states and the flower of Ohio's state tree—the buckeye—smells too much. We are not sure where McKinley got his carnations, since he could not just go out to the flower patch behind his garage and pick some, but he liked to wear a red carnation in his lapel at public events and the state legislature designated the red carnation as the Official State Flower to honor him. It is the only state to choose that particular flower. In fact, no other state has a carnation of any color at all as its Official State Flower. It is also interesting that the state flag of Ohio is the only one (out of fifty) without a single right angle to its border, although that probably is not McKinley's fault.

The next President named William also came from Ohio. This alone is not surprising since Ohio calls itself "mother of Presidents." She produced eight presidents. But so did Virginia. None of the Virginia presidents, however, were as great, as in great in size, as president #27, **William Howard Taft**. No other president from anywhere, for that matter, was as big as William Taft. At six feet tall, 340 pounds, with a body mass index of 46 he was, well, simply big. So big, in fact, that he was called a "walrus in wingtips." Most of his other nicknames had something to do with his bulk: "Big Lub," "Big Bill," "Big Will," and— figure this one out— "Sleeping Beauty." Actually, it is easily explained, for an unfortunate side effect of his obesity was a tendency to fall asleep—just brief little catnaps, mind you—during official government meetings. There were reports of him dozing off at the theater, at church, at funerals, even in an open convertible parading down Fifth Avenue in Manhattan. He even fell asleep once during a performance of *Die Meistersinger von Nurnberg,* a five-and-a-quarter hour opera by **Wilhelm Richard Wagner**. Imagine doing that!

His blood pressure was high; he gasped for breath when climbing the Capitol steps or getting up from a chair. His heart weakened from trying to circulate oxygenated blood around to all parts of his bulk. At the insistence of his doctors he went on a diet regimen similar to what is now called a Mediterranean diet, and lost seventy pounds. He was down to a sylphlike 270 pounds by the time of his death. William Howard Taft, "The Great One."

Our last president William is the only one we called "Bill": #42, **William Jefferson Clinton**. He was in office eight years and could be remembered for accomplishing a great number of things, like

inheriting a deficit and leaving a surplus,

like

creating 22 million new jobs,

like

raising education standards

and like a whole bunch of other good things, but what he seems to be most remembered for is not what he did while sitting at the desk in the Oval Office but for what was going on under it. Rumor has it, and there were lots of rumors, that sometimes he would be communicating orally by telephone with foreign ambassadors while a young White House intern named Monica was crawling around under the desk giving targeted oral massage to his body parts, one part in particular.

During his term

welfare rolls were the lowest they had been in three decades.

But that's not what people remember about him. The Monica thing was more interesting., even though he was president during

> *the longest period of economic expansion in American history*

he is remembered for his extramarital dalliances. Those, more than the fact that

> *he added 100,000 more cops to police our streets,*

probably accounted for the fact that he left office with the

> *highest approval rating of any departing president since Harry Truman.*

When talking about Clinton many folks say he should have been impeached. Well, he was. He just was not removed from office as a result of impeachment proceedings. That's because impeachment and removal are not the same thing. Impeachment proceedings start in the House, but it takes the Senate to find guilt (or acquittal and removal.) He was the second president in U.S. history to be brought before the House for impeachment hearings. Andrew Johnson was the first, way back in 1868, just after the Civil War. In the Johnson case there were eleven charges; he was acquitted in the Senate of all of them.

In the Clinton case there were only two. The charges were not directly involved with the Monica-related behavior, but with perjury and obstruction of justice. Like Johnson 130 years before, Clinton, who

connected ninety-five percent of American schools to the internet

was acquitted in the Senate.

Richard Nixon, "Tricky Dick," was never impeached. The issue about him involved five guys snooping around the office of the Democratic national headquarters with flashlights one night in the Watergate office building in Washington. It is not exactly clear what exactly they were looking for, but it became obvious that they had been hired by the Committee to Re-elect the President (who was Nixon.) That was not a good thing to do. A cover-up was involved and there were denials and accusations. It was a fellow named Bill who most people have never heard of that provided enough leaks to the press to turn public opinion against the president. Facing almost certain impeachment (the guilty-as-charged and subsequent removal from office kind,) Nixon resigned. So, for a long time there had been only two impeachments ever— Andrew Johnson and Bill Clinton. Then came Donald Trump, who was impeached twice during his single frantic term of office.

The reason people had not heard of the fellow who provided the Watergate leaks in the Clinton impeachment case, at least at the time, is that he was only known by the nickname "Deep Throat." It wasn't until after his death thirty-one years later that he was identified as Mark Felt. Not a Bill, you notice? That's because the name given to him at birth was **William Mark Felt**. Somewhere in his youth he must have dropped the William part. The "Deep Throat" nickname came from the most popular porn film of the time, possibly the most popular porn film ever. Or maybe he just had a gravely, deep voice.

And when it comes to name droppers, Bill Clinton himself is a good example.; his last name was not always Clinton.

His grandfather's name was: **William Jefferson Blythe**.

His father's name: **William Jefferson Blythe, Jr**.

#42: **William Jefferson Blythe III**.

What, you've never heard of President Blythe? That's because his father, Blythe, Jr., an auto-parts salesman in Arkansas, died in an automobile accident three months before the baby was born. The mother remarried when William III was seven years old and he took the Clintonian surname of his stepfather. He's been Bill Clinton ever since, with lots of nicknames, like "Slick Willie," "Big Dog," and just plain "Bubba."

So there they are—four President Bills— "Old Tippecanoe," "Wobbly Willie," "Big Will," and "Slick Willie." Remembered for, in chronological order: supporting the gold standard, for being assassinated, for being fat, and for having an affair with an intern in the oval office. Which carried a nickname of its own: "The Oval Orifice," or "The Oral Office."

There are three things you just can't do in life. You can't beat the phone company, you can't make a waiter see you until he's ready to see you, and you can't go home again.
—*Bill Bryson*

"Bills! Bills! Bills!"

That is the opening line, at least in a popular English translation, of a 1673 play by French playwright Molière called, in English, *The Imaginary Invalid*. It's about a grumpy, aristocratic hypochondriac. As the curtain opens he is seated at his desk opening his daily mail. He's having a fit. Deep sighs. Moaning exhales. Exaggerated theatrical gestures that communicate "Alas, oh me, oh welladay." What's in his mail today? Bills! Bills! Bills! He is not talking about guys named Bill, or the French equivalent Guillaume; he is looking at lower-case b bills. His illnesses might not be real ones, but those invoices from his health care providers are. If the play were performed in French he would have complained, with much sighing and groaning, "*Les additions! Les additions! Les additions!*"

The French word actually makes more sense than the English, for a statement of accounts is indeed really an addition—a summing up of items or services that need to be paid for. It would make more sense in an American restaurant to ask the waiter for a totalling-up statement rather than for a bill, which is something you might pull out of your wallet to pay with. The Germans call it, *die Rechnung*, a term that acknowledges the thing as some sort of reckoning. In Spain it's *la cuenta*. In Italy, *il conto*. In Portugal, *a conta*. All of which suggest some sort of counting up. Interesting, though, that in Wales, where it takes the whole mouthful of "biwyddyn Newydd flyddyn I chi" just to wish somebody a happy new year, the word for the bill is almost disappointing. It is, simply: *bil*.

The hard part of paying the bill in a restaurant is often just *getting it* in the first place. It is hard to call *le garcon* if you don't speak French, hard to catch the eye of *el mesero* if you don't speak Spanish, and always tough to summon *il cameriere* whether you can do Italian or not. Italian waiters undergo years of training in avoidance of requests from diners eager to pay up and get out of there. In Provence you can grow *une barbe* while awaiting *l'addition*; in Portugal you can make your own coal. But there is one universally understood language to indicate that you are ready for the bill—it's a gesture. Pretend that you are writing on the palm of your hand. If that doesn't work there is always communication by pulling out your wallet, removing a few bills, and waving them in the air. Money talks.

Consider those bills in your wallet. Be glad they are there. Before anybody figured out the idea of paper money they used the bartering system. If you were a farmer and had lots of corn, lots of milk, or lots of chickens, or even lots of manure, and you wanted to buy something like, say, a pair of boots, you would load your wagon with a half dozen or so flappping hens, a few jugs of milk, and definitely a generous supply of horse manure and then head into to city to make a deal. You would locate a shoemaker with a family who needs milk. Or one that needs a chicken for dinner. Or manure for his small city garden.

"I'll give you four gallons of milk for those boots."

"Four gallons of milk? No way. These boots are made of genuine horse leather."

"Four gallons plus a hen. And the milk was fresh this morning."

"Four gallons and TWO hens."

"How about five gallons and one hen?"

"TWO hens."

"I really like those boots. Tell you what; I'll give you five gallons of milk, one hen, and I'll toss in two shovelfuls of horseshit."

"THREE shovelfuls."

"Two. This stuff comes from thoroughbreds and it's well-rotted. Quality shit."

"DONE!"

And with that, you've acquired the boots you coveted but you still need to cart all of those unspent chickens and manure back home. Likewise, the shoe guy also has to lug all that stuff home. You get the idea: paper money is easier. To wit:

"How much you want for those boots?"

"Ninety-six ninety-nine."

"Cool. Got change for a Benjamin?"

With that simple exchange the deal is done. Nobody needs to cart anything cumbersome anywhere. You can even wear the boots home if you want. But the paper money system only works if the paper is actually *worth* something and as a piece of paper it is not intrinsically worth much at all. A nickel, perhaps, since that is close to what it costs the government to print a one dollar bill. For years paper money was issued as a Silver Certificate, with a note at the bottom claiming obligation to pay a dollar's worth of silver to its bearer when he takes it to the bank and demands it. That practice stopped in 1964, perhaps because it became too awkward to keep all that silver on hand ready to meet demands from all those "bearers" or perhaps because nobody knew where to go to make the demand. Your local bank? The Federal Reserve, wherever that is? Fort Knox?

Anyway, paper money no longer promises that it can be exchange for actual silver. Now they are printing what are called Federal Reserve Notes and, whether we understand the most basic tenets of economics—gross domestic product, purchasing power parity, gross mixed income, and all of those concepts that are usually referenced by acronyms (GNP, PPP, GMI, etc., that are meaningful to folks with acronyms after their names, like CFP, CFA, CPA, CMA, MBA, or WTF) —we all seem to understand that a dollar bill is worth a dollar. And we trust the Federal Reserve to agree with us.

Pull out a dollar bill and let's explore it. Feel it. There is a special "feel" to it, right? That's because not all paper is alike. Charmin is not the same as The New York Times; the stack of paper in your printer is not the same as National Geographic. The paper in all of those is made from wood pulp. No trees at all are used in making paper money; it is 75% cotton from cotton plants and 25% linen from flax plants. That's what gives it that special feel and makes it durable. Nothing, of course, lasts forever; the life span of a typical dollar bill is about a year and a half. Then it is shredded and recycled into roofing shingles.

There are two signatures on it, those of the Secretary of the Treasury and of the Treasurer or the United States. They are not the same person. There have been 77 Secretaries of The Treasury. Eleven of them were Williams. Forty-four Treasurers; only four were Bills. But it doesn't matter greatly because you can't read the signatures of most of them anyway. Why is it that the more important the signer, the less legible the signature? With one exception: Donald Trump's Secretary of the Treasury, Steven T. Mnuchin printed his in block letters. A second grader could read it.

There is no question about how much your dollar bill is worth. Count up all the times it tells you—all the times you can find the English word "one" and all the Arabic number "1's." How many did you find?[*]

---

[*] There are sixteen.

You will also find some Roman numbers, a whole string of them—MDCCLXVI— which is Latin for 1776. There are also some Latin phrases: *Novus Ordo Seculorum,* meaning "a new order through the ages," *E Pluribus Unum,* "From many, one," and *Annuit Coeptis,* "God has favored our undertaking." It should be greatly reassuring to know we have divine approval. Even the Egyptians have a presence on the green side of the bill. That pyramid is supposed to indicate strength and ability to weather the ages. Odd, isn't it, that the top part of it seems to be separated from the bottom and hovering in its own aura of light above it. The better, perhaps, for that eye to look out over the desert.

The number thirteen is supposed to be unlucky. It never appears as such on a dollar bill but there are thirteen arrows and thirteen olives in in the eagle's talons, thirteen stars above the eagle's head, thirteen vertical bars on his shield, and thirteen steps on the pyramid. All of that is because back when the country got started in MDCCLXVI there were XIII colonies. From those came *unum.*

Probably the most obvious feature of any of our bills, no matter what denomination, is a portrait of a dead person. The Secretary of the Treasury is the one who decides whose portrait is to appear. The only criteria specified are that they must be "persons whose place in history the American people know well" and they have to be dead. The first of those criteria might be subject to debate but there should be no question about the other. Federal law prohibits likeness of any living person. Most of the portraits are of dead presidents. Two exceptions: Alexander Hamilton and Benjamin Franklin. Not to worry, their place in history is indeed well known.

Now if you still have that dollar bill in your hand, look at the ink. Tip the bill slightly fore and aft and side to side under good light. Sorry, but nothing happens. Do the same thing, though, with a $20 bill and watch what happens to the 20's in the lower corner—see how they change color? That adds a major hurdle to anyone trying to print up a garageful of fake $20 bills. Try the same experiment with a $100 bill and watch how those bells dance from up and down. Try *that,* counterfeiter!

One of the dumbest things about American paper money is that it's all the same size. Sure, it's convenient to know that if you need to measure something and don't have handy access to a yardstick or a tape measure you can simply pull out a bill of any random denomination knowing it is six inches wide (well, 6.14 inches to be exact) but when it comes to paying in cash for something that one-size-fits-all dimension won't be of any use at all to a blind person. In other countries, though, the money comes not only in different colors for each denomination, but different sizes as well.

The U.S-Mexico border measures 1,954 miles from the Pacific Ocean to the Gulf of Mexico. If you laid dollar bills end to end it would take 20,634,240 of them to cover that distance. Costing, of course, $20,634,240. The smallest note the Mexicans print is their 20 peso bill, which measures 4.724 inches. Being shorter than a dollar, it would take more of them to reach ocean-to ocean. 26,2077,756 of them, to be exact. But since pesos are worth only about 1/25 of a dollar, those 26-odd million 20-peso bills lying along the border are worth only $1,048,310, or roughly twenty times less than an equivalent length of dollars. That's a lot of calculations, yes, but there is a moral: It would be cheaper to build a wall in pesos. So let the Mexicans pay for it.

Not all bills have anything to do with money. There have been bills of various types ever since paper and ink were invented. During the Black Plague of London in the 1600's weekly notices listing names of that week's dead—*bills* of mortality—were posted. In London today, or in practically anywhere that anybody can find room to put up a notice, public wall spaces are cluttered with overlapping bills promoting everything from psychic readings and rock concerts to rewards for lost Fidos and Fluffies or used cars and motorcycles for sale. Most of them are way past their "sell by" date, plugging events that happened months ago. Apparently, there is more enthusiasm for posting new bills than there is for removing tattered old ones. The same thing happens on bulletin boards in college dorm hallways or community senior centers. In an effort to control the resultant clutter, inviting wall spaces often include a bill of warning that reads POST NO BILLS. It is generally ignored and cluttered with overlapping, often outdated, posted bills.

The big ones along the highway are called billboards. Most people do not like them, but they do seem to work. When driving a long distance, it is of course useful to learn of a restaurant coming up in a few miles. Or a hotel. Or someplace that sounds like it might have a bathroom. But it is hard to see how an 8 x 22 foot portrait of a middle-aged personal injury lawyer is going to improve your trip. Generally, billboards are considered eyesores. That's is why they are not permitted at all in four of our most scenic states—Alaska, Hawaii, Maine, and Vermont, all of whom realize that unblemished scenery brings more tourist dollars into their economies than what great big ads for car dealerships and law firms. Other states restrict their number and distance from the roadway. By federal law there can be no more than 26 of them along any single mile of Interstate highway and only 106 per mile on primary urban roadways. 106 per mile, That's one every fifty feet!

The most successful outdoor advertising campaign **ever** did not use huge billboards. It used little signs—about eight inches high and about two feet wide. Red, with words printed in white uppercase block letters. Their message was a short verse or jingle, usually light-hearted and humorous. They were posted in series of six with a few words of the jingle on each one and were placed just far enough apart so that readers in a car traveling approximately 35-40 mph could read them in sequence. The last sign in the series bore the name of the company, Burma-Shave, in script.

Burma-Shave? It is no longer around. Nor are the signs. But they were familiar along most roadways in America from 1926 to 1963. The Burma-Shave product was a brushless shave cream; this was before the pressurized cans of foam we use today.

Some examples:

Burma-Shave

ITCHY FACE

FINDS AN

IF SHE FINDS

NO KISSY-FACE

THERE WILL BE

Burma-Shave

TEXT WHILE DRIVING

IF YOU TRY TO

ARRIVING

YOU ARE

TELL ST. PETE

Ok, those are made up. You knew that because obviously there was no texting while driving back in the Burma-Shave era. The real ones are copyrighted but you can find all 600 of them in Frank Rowsome, Jr.'s book *The Verse by the Side of the Road: The Story of the Burma-Shave Signs* without driving anywhere. Those little signs were in their heyday nearly a hundred years ago and people in their retirement years now still remember them and talk about them. There are a few posted along Route 66 in Arizona as a sort of living history exhibition but otherwise they are gone from our roadsides. A few can still be found in a handful of transportation-related museums scattered about the country. Plus the Smithsonian. Those little signs worked because speeds were slow. As cars got faster and highways improved signs had to become bigger to be effective. That is what gave us those behemoth billboards we see today. Does anyone really think that when the current crop of young people reaches their own eighties and nineties they will remember a billboard they glanced at while passing at 75mph long ago? Especially one for a personal injury lawyer? It is a pity that POST NO BILLS does not apply to billboards.

Years ago, back in the Burma-Shave days when schools taught civics, there was always a section on How A Bill Becomes a Law. It included a full-page flow chart showing how an idea conceived by one smiling representative went to a smiling committee and then to a full congressional vote. Then to the other house. Then to the president, who could either sign it, tear it up, or—they call this the "pocket veto" — he could stuff it in his pocket and forget about it. It looked so easy, with all of those people so happy as they carried the bill through the various steps and arrows of the flow chart but it did not make a whole lot of sense. We learned about the concept of a "bicameral legislature" and thought that meant it included a camel with two humps. We learned about "the filibuster" where one person could hog the microphone as long as he could until he needed to pee so urgently that he would bust. Civics is not taught in schools today, at least not as a distinct unit, although most schools manage to sneak a bit of it into Social Studies. They have twelve years to do that in, and if they did, that unit could be called How a Bill Becomes a Flaw.

We also learned, sort of, about the Bill of Rights. Well, okay, that's an upper-case *B* example, but it's still not a human Bill or William. It included promises for a free press, but of course we still had to pay for the local newspaper. It included the right not to be forced to cut soldiers into quarters or to suffer seizures. We could have bare arms if the militia, whatever that is, was properly regulated. And they can't make you go on Jeopardy twice.

The whole idea of the Bill of Rights was to keep the government from selling you a bill of goods. A "bill of goods?" It sounds like something innocuous like a receipt or an invoice for a list of stuff, but then we learned later that if somebody sells you a bill of goods you've been had. Hoodwinked, swindled. A bill of goods would be listed in Bill of Wrongs.

Bills! Bills! Bills! You can't avoid them. Go to a diner and they've posted a *bill of fare*. Buy a car and they give you a *bill of sale*. Truckers have a *bill of lading* when they start off with a full shipment and then a *bill of delivery* when the unload. Borrow money and you have to sign a *bill of exchange*. See your doctor and hope for a clean bill of health. Then, of course, we have the daily mail—electric bills, insurance bills, Mastercard bills, doctor bills, cable bills, trash bills, mortgage bills, monthly bills, what-the-hell's-*this* bills, goddamned bills—Bills! Bills! Bills!

When birds burp, it must taste like bugs.
—Bill Watterson

One End of a Chicken

Ever notice how many birds are named for something about their bills? Take spoonbills, for instance. Their bills look like spoons. Or crossbills. The two parts of their bills cross over each other. Grossbeaks have big bills; some folks would call them gross. Shoebills have what look like wooden shoes. Sometimes the names get more descriptive— like the ivory-billed woodpecker, the ring-billed gull, the paint-billed crake, or the black-billed magpie. The long-billed curlew. The groove-billed ani.

There is a reason for all of those names: it is simply because birds don't hold still. A botanist can study a pressed flower as closely as he wishes and can take a long time doing it. Likewise a geologist studying rocks. But the bird folks get only a fleeting—blink your eyes and you missed it—glimpse as the objects of their attention flit from tree to tree; they have to name their subjects for something really obvious, like the spoon-shaped bill or whatever, something they can observe in an instant.

Sure, lots of birds are named for lots of parts other than their bills, like the red-winged blackbird (a black bird with red wing bars) or the scissor-tailed flycatcher (a bird that catches flies and has a scissor-shaped tail.) Or the greater yellowlegs and the lesser yellowlegs. (One is bigger than the other but both have yellow legs.) The short-eared owl. The black-capped chickadee. When it comes to body parts, there seems to be significant fixation on breasts: the red-breasted merganser, the yellow-breasted chat, the buff-breasted sandpiper, or the lilac-breasted roller. The easiest way to tell a red-breasted nuthatch from a white-breasted nuthatch or a brown-breasted one is by the color of their breasts. But do not confuse breasts with boobies, at least not in the world of birds. There are blue-footed boobies, red-footed boobies, brown boobies, and masked boobies. Those names have nothing to do with their breasts.

Also, do not confuse breasts with tits. Sure, there are great tits. There are also blue tits and brown tits. And long-tailed tits. In general, boobies are medium-sized, web-footed birds of the tropics and tits are wee wren-like creatures of North America.

Then there are cocks—woodcocks, gamecocks, peacocks. In England, at the recommendation of the Royal Society for Protection of Birds, avian males are not called cocks. Instead, they are replaced as **** in printed text. The Brits, however, have no qualms about boobies and tits. They write about them, talk about them, even sing about them. One of the most popular songs from Gilbert and Sullivan's *The Mikado*, way back in 1885, tells a wistful, sad tale of a lovelorn willow tit.

Some people are very fond of cocks. They brag about the biggest and best-looking ones and enter them in competitions at county and state fairs. At Harrisburg's annual Pennsylvania Farm Show there are awards for cocks in two categories—one is for large poultry and the other is for Bantams. The entrance fee for Bantams is fifty cents cheaper—smaller cocks. There is a blue ribbon for Best Cock. And a red ribbon for Runner Up Cock. Of course the award plaques do not specifically use that exact terminology, but the winners (not the cocks themselves, but their owners/exhibitors, especially 4-H Club teen-ages for whom poultry exhibition is a gateway endeavor leading into work with larger animals like cattle and swine, use those terms when they get back home to the farm.

But some cocks are among the most hated creatures in the world. Surely you have heard them. Suppose you have spent months anticipating a relaxing week on a Caribbean island, a respite from the urban rat race and perhaps a mid-winter warm-up. You have found what sounds like the ideal B&B with a view of the ocean from a "bucolic hillside setting." The day of travel getting there has been exhausting—that glitch at airport security, the two-hour flight delay, five hours in a seat two inches narrower than your butt, the fuckup about the luggage, the hassle with the cab driver, and arrival too late for dinner. You have missed the sunset from that bucolic view. You fall into bed but, as tired as you are, you are too keyed up to fall asleep. Eventually you doze off, or at least a few minutes go missing from your all-too-regular checks of the beside clock. And then it happens. Somewhere outside your open window the very first photon of the day, one that has taken eight minutes and twenty seconds to get from the sun to your bucolic island setting, one that hardly counts as dawn yet, stirs a goddamned rooster. One photon;

that's all it takes. *Cock-a-doodle-do! Cock-a-doodle-do! Cock-a-doodle-do!* Thus begins Day One of your Caribbean week. Only six more mornings until you can go back to the office. Or at least to some place where there are no cocks in the morning.

Contrary to popular rumor, Ogden Nash never said:

> *A wonderful bird is the pelican.*
> *His bill can hold more than his belly can.*
> *For in his beak he can hold food for a week*
> *And I don't see how in hellican.*

The are several things wrong with that. For one, when a pelican catches a fish he doesn't store it in his bill. It goes into a throat pouch. And a full pouch of fish won't hold a pelican for a full week. He will need a fresh catch-of-the-day every day. The other thing wrong is that it wasn't Ogden Nash, the mostly Baltimore "Candy is dandy but liquor is quicker" poet. It was a Tennessee newspaper editor named Dixon Merritt.

Biologically, bills are amazing. We know that birds evolved from dinosaur-like precursors because we have found fossil records to prove that. Go to the dinosaur exhibit in whatever Museum of Natural History is nearest your home and one thing you will notice immediately about the dinosaur skeletons exhibited there are the teeth. Not only are they prominent; they are also plentiful. Contemporary birds, however, do not have teeth at all. Somewhere in the process of evolving from dinos to birds the teeth gradually shrank away to oblivion while the bills grew larger and larger. And just as certain teeth are good for performing specific functions, like molars for grinding and incisors for cutting, different bills are good for different jobs. Pointy, wedge-shaped bills are good for eating seeds, spoons are best for scooping up algae, and daggers serve well for stabbing fish or frogs. The right tool for the job.

Darwin made that observation way back in 1835 when his *HMS Beagle* pulled into the Galapagos Islands, about 1,000 miles west of the Ecuador coast. He observed that the finches on different islands ate different diets because different plants predominated on different islands. The bills on the finches, too, differed from one island to another. The bills on islands where cacti and fruits were available were broader than the pointy bills on islands where seeds were more available.

Darwin figured that a few families of ur-finches, all from the same breeding stock, somehow managed to get from the mainland over to the islands and set up dynasties there. Slight variations in bill structure favored some birds over others and those best-adapted to the food supplies on hand reproduced more vigorously than the birds that were not quite so blessed. Hence, over time, the forces of **natural selection** and **survival of the fittest** prevailed. The fourteen species of finches in the Galapagos Islands all look pretty much alike except for those different bills. Darwin, as biologists do, gave them Latin names based on some identifiable characteristic. Usually it was their bill, as in *Camarrhynchus parylulus* "heavy cone-shaped bill" or *Platyspiza crassirostris* "flat-billed broad finch." For people who speak fluent Latin or even passable Biology the names are useful. The finch with the flat bill is the one that eats leaves. It is also called the "vegetarian finch." As a vegetarian it would probably be happy on an island with nothing but kale and quinoa, but in the Galapagos it has to settle for cacti. The other one eats seeds. Form follows function.

Bird-watchers see that everywhere. Look at the ducks with their algae-scooping spoons. Look at the goldfinches with their tweezers for picking up seeds. Look at the flat triangles of birds that eat flies. Look at the pliers of crossbills that can open pine cones. Or the ice picks of herons that catch fish. Each adaptation would be useless if faced with the wrong food source. Just imagine trying to scoop up a meal of pond scum with a dagger or trying to spear a frog with a spoon. Form follows food.

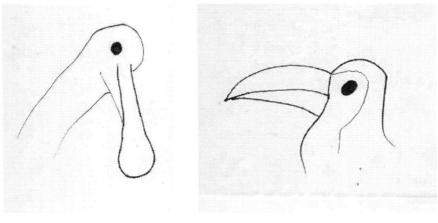

Spoonbill   Toucan

Biochemically, the bills of birds are built from a type of protein called keratin. It is the same stuff their feathers and claws are made of. We humans make it too—our toenails, our hair, even one layer of our skin. But birds have managed to do things with their bills that we cannot even fathom doing with our toenails. There are no yuppy bill salons located in strip malls nor do birds apply a full spectrum of colored bill polish three times a week. No, birds just stick with the same bill "look" they were hatched with for their entire lives. Those bills seem to serve as needed without external assistance.

The bills of hummingbirds are great examples, for they can probe the deepest recesses of the narrowest flowers in search of nectar. The tiny hummers do not slurp up nectar using their bills like soda straws. Their tongues are long, narrow, and forked at the end. When they sense the sweetness at the bottom of a flower tube the forks separate and then close again, trapping a sampling of the nectar. It happens really fast. We're talking nanoseconds here. It's an ingenious mechanism. They can drink up to eight times their body weight in nectar in a single day. But remember, the hummingbird is not very heavy to start with. He weighs about three grams; if he were made entirely of marijuana he would provide only enough for about half a dozen decent-sized joints.

The bills and tongues of woodpeckers are even more remarkable, especially when you consider that all of that high-frequency jackhammering echoing through the woods is just a feeding mechanism. Surely it would be easier to grab a fork, as humans have been doing since the fork was invented in the fourth century, to pick up dinner, even if that dinner is insects. But without opposable thumbs, birds have to do everything with their bills. Woodpeckers included. The pickaxe point of the woodpecker bill is effective in piercing through the bark of the tree but it does not stab the insect prey. It is the tongue that brings the harvest home. The woodpecker tongue is so long that it coils around behind the brain—okay, so it's only a birdbrain—inside the skull. In that ever-so-brief moment when the bill is at the bottom of the hole the tongue is whipped out to grab the bug. The speed is mind-boggling, at least to the human brain.

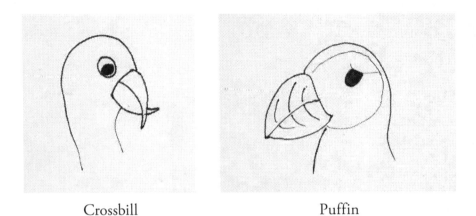

Crossbill   Puffin

If you have never seen a toucan in the wild you have probably seen one in a zoo. They are the big tropical birds with humongous orange bills—bills so big that you wonder how they can walk around lugging them everywhere they go, let alone how they could possibly take off and fly. At about eight inches long, the bill makes up nearly a third of the bird's total length. There must be some advantage to such front-heavy protuberances or, according to Darwin and two additional centuries of biologists, they would not exist. They are useless when attempting to pluck a mango from a tree and not much help in building nests. They have nothing to do with attracting mates; a lady toucan cares not a tweet about the size of a male's bill.

Researchers have found evidence for something those bills actually accomplish: thermoregulation. In other words, they act as radiators.

When people get hot they sweat. When dogs get hot they pant. When toucans get hot they radiate. A typical toucan bill has about forty square inches of surface area, roughly equivalent to a rolled-up page from Readers Digest, all of it smooth and unfeathered. Just as a homeowner can control the temperature of his rooms by regulating the flow of hot water through his radiators, the hot toucan can control his whole cooling process by regulating by the rate of blood flowing just below the surface. He is probably not aware of doing it.

Even bigger than the toucan bill is that of the hornbill, especially on the ones called "Rhinoceros hornbills" The black and white birds themselves are large, but it is their gigantic bright orange and yellow bills they are famous for. The top part of the bill has a big lumpy protrusion—hence the "rhinocerous" reference—that looks almost like a second bill. Or a tumor. It is called as casque. The whole thing appears thoroughly unwieldly; how could any bird survive lugging that thing around in the jungle night and day? Truth is, it is actually hollow and very light; they could not do without it. With it they can puck fruits from the jungle and scoop up small creatures like mice. But the tongue is too short to swallow the prey properly so he has to jerk his head back to toss his dinner back into the workable part of his throat, the way some people do when they have trouble swallowing pills.

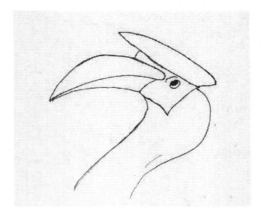

Hornbill

The "horn" part of the hornbill name might derive from that loud honking, that gododawfullest loud quacking they do. It can be heard from three miles away. It's a far cry from the gentle billing and cooing of their smaller kin.

But one of the most important, and weirdest, functions of the hornbill's megabill is involved in their nesting behavior. When it is time to lay a clutch of eggs lady hornbill builds a nest in a cavity in a tree and then covers the opening with a wall of mud and begins a period of solitary confinement. This allows her to keep the hatchlings safe from predators. She leaves a narrow slit, just wide enough for her to push waste out from the nest and for the male to bring her and the chicks food until they are deemed big enough to go out on their own. When the time is right she uses her big bill to bash her way out of the mudwall. The young'uns fly away immediately for life in the jungle. And ladybird has to find her own dinners again.

Lady peacocks (peahens), lady grouses, and lots of other lady birds get turned on by male displays like "Just look at these tail feathers," and

"Look how big my chest is," or "Watch this new hip-hop step I can do."
But there are of course some birds who do seem to get turned on by large
bills, especially if they are colorful. The Atlantic puffin—those cute,
chunky black and white birds clamoring in colonies of hundreds around
offshore rocks and covering them with their bodies, their raucous cries,
and their voluminous poop. Because of their amusing behavior and
the size and prominence of their red and yellow bills they have earned
nicknames like "sea parrot" and "clown of the sea." In their northern
Atlantic habitat they certainly do not need those large bills for radiation
as the tropical toucan does. The edges of their bills are serrated like a
saw blade to help them hold as many as a dozen slippery fish at once;
perhaps that provided a selective advantage tilting in favor of evolving
such large bills. When breeding season comes around the bills develop
bright red plates, making them appear larger and, apparently, at least as
viewed by other puffins, sexier. It seems to work, for even though they
produce only one egg per nest, their population numbers are staggering

Birds are not the only creatures that have bills. In the field of biology
there is an entire taxonomic Order of fishes, the Order Istiophoriformes
("carriers of sail-shapes"), with long bony snouts. Their nickname, the
billfish, pretty much describes them. Among the more familiar examples
are swordfish, sailfish, spearfish, and marlin. Just as ornithologists name
their birds because of something about their bills, ichthyologists also
name their billfish on the same principals. Hence, we have longbilled
spearfish as well as shortbilled spearfish. Swordfish appear on menus
in even the fanciest of restaurants, but most of the other billfish are

more likely to appear stuffed, or whatever taxidermists do to them, and mounted on walls of manly sportsclubs and other mancaves as trophies. Who remembers why that old man in Hemmingway's novel pursued that big marlin—it certainly was not due to hunger.

The function of the billfish bill is to catch prey. A spearfish swims through a school of smaller fish like anchovies or sardines while swinging his bill left and right, occasionally stabbing an *hors d'oeuvre*, just as the fellows attending an after-fishing party might stab an anchovy with a toothpick. We know how the fisherman gets the nibble up to his mouth; he has a bendable arm and a flexible thumb to help with that. But how, one wonders, does a spearfish without arms and fingers get the anchovy off the tip of his spear and into his mouth?

We generally do not think of mammals as having bills. But in the eastern corner of Australia and in the most bizarre corner of mammaldom are strange amphibious creatures known as duck-billed platypuses. Since they are actually the *only* platypuses (platypi?) alive today they really do not need to be labelled specifically as "duck-billed" at all but that does describe one of their most unusual features. Recall that old story about the blind men and the elephant. Each one had a different idea of what an elephant looks like based upon which part of the elephant he touched. The one who felt only the tail was sure that an elephant is like a rope. The trunk guy thought an elephant is like a tree branch. The belly—a wall; the ear—a fan. That committee of blind men would have a heyday if they were to try to assess the platypus! The one who touched the lips would certainly think he'd encountered a duck. The fellow who touched the tail would know he had a beaver.

The feet—webbed like an otter. The toenails—thorns from a rose bush. If one of them happened to be scratched by one of those claws he would cry out in immediate pain from the venom, a poisonous defense against platypus enemies. Humans who experienced this venom have claimed they would have preferred a bullet. As mammals, platypuses would be expected to give birth to live young. But instead, these mammals lay eggs. Like birds or turtles. Like a seal, they are athletic and graceful in water but on land they are clumsy. When they were first discovered and reports made their way back to Europe people thought it was an attention-grabbing hoax. Who would ever believe such a hodgepodge creature could be real? They are not real pretty. Just really weird.

Scientists have recently discovered another weird thing about platypuses—their fur glows under ultraviolet light like those rocks in natural history museums, or a few other living creatures like those cute puffins pooping on rocky shores, and lots of squishy jellyfish. Several theories have been put forth to account for what-on-earth possible kind of selective advantage this fluorescent trait bestows on the species but nobody really knows for sure. One thing for sure: if a platypus waddles into a disco bar with UV lights illuminating the dance floor he will indeed attract attention; he will have "that glow."

On pretty much every pond in every park in every town in America you find lots of ducks. Most of them are mallards. Their biological name is *Anas platyrhynchos*. The *Anas* part is simply Biology for "duck" and it safest not to attempt to pronounce it in public unless absolutely necessary, like "Johnny, you've got to stop throwing bread to those

Anases. You might fall in." The *platyrhynchos* part means "flat bill," exactly the sort of tool any self-respecting bird needs for scooping ripped slabs of soggy bread from the surface of a city park pond. Except for the opalescent green heads of the males, the rest of the ducks—both genders—-are mostly a drab brown. But when they were babies, all fuzzy and Easter basket yellow, there was nothing cuter. Well, maybe kittens.

Mommy duck sat on her fertilized eggs for twenty-eight days until the wee things started to peck their way out of their confining shells. In grade school science classes we have watched baby chickens hatch under the warmth of a sixty-watt light bulb; first a tiny crack appears in the eggshell and we see the pointy bill of the chick. It must be more difficult for duckies with those flat *platyrynchos* bills. Anyone who has ever tried to bash through the seal on a bottle of vitamin pills knows that a knife point works better than a spoon. Perhaps that is why it takes a baby duck a full twenty-four hours to chip his way out. But once out of the shell, all those babies need to do is take a little time to dry out and then mommy leads them in an orderly line to water where they begin what they will do for the rest of their lives—eat, swim, quack, and poop.

The other birds we see on pretty much every pond in every park, at least in the east, is the Canada goose. Yes, the Canada goose (not Canadian.) They are not just on ponds but also on lawns, golf courses, football fields, landscaped parks, post-harvest crop fields—pretty much anywhere where there is grass. Their populations are legion. They are a problem.

Each adult goose eats four pounds of grass every day and excretes three pounds of poop. For comparison, a hippopotamus eats eighty-eight pounds and poops four hundred pounds. But he is bigger than a goose and his poop is mostly liquid. So what he does in the water all day is drink water and poop; he comes out to eat grass at night. It is those three pounds of poop per goose that gives the entire Canada goose population its bad reputation. At some venues where outdoor weddings are held the management has to hire someone with a power washer to come and clean the grass about an hour before the guests arrive. That's one more thing for the wedding coordinator to take care of, for we can't have the bride or—worse yet, the bride's mother—stepping in goose poop.

People try very creative methods to keep the Canada goose population at bay, using everything from plastic coyotes, electric fences, laser beams, explosives, even Border Collies. The National Park Service hires a contractor to keep the Canada goose off the National Mall in Washington. It is nothing against Canada, just anti-goose poop.

It is our own fault that there is so much goose poop, for we are the ones that caused the goose population explosion. Actually, the goose population is *two* populations. There was the native Canada goose, *Branta canadensis* (that's Biology for "goose from Canada") that migrates in those spectacular V-formations in the autumn sky. They don't stay around all year. By the end of the 19th century the native population had declined because of human activities like egg collecting, overhunting and encroachment into wetland habitats. In 1930 the government released a new type, the "giant" Canada goose for hunting. Some people also brought them in as decorative additions to their ponds on golf courses or industrial parks.

Like many living things into new regions, their population exploded. (A good example is dandelions.) It seems that we could control the non-natives by allowing a seasonal hunt for them. Trouble is, the natives are protected by the Migratory Bird Treaty Act and both populations look pretty much alike at least to us. They share the same territory but do not interbreed, so the birds must be able to tell each other apart and mate only with their own kind. They pair up for life with one partner; it is amazing how they can find him/her out of the hundred birds that might be pooping on the same lawn. They live up to thirty years. Think about that: thirty years at three pounds of poop per day. That works out to fifteen tons of poop per goose. And that's only one goose! Our Mother Goose books, when we were little, never told about the volume of her output. Yes, even Mother Goose poops.

So we have several duck-billed nuisances, but a fascinating thing about ducks and geese is concerned about what happens at the other end of the bird—farthest away from the bill. In adaptation to flight with its requirement to decrease weight, birds do not excrete liquid urine. Their waste, from both digestive and circulatory system sources, leave the body from a common opening. They do not control excretion the way humans and dogs—at least well-trained dogs—do; they just release waste periodically as the spirit moves them, which is about every twenty minutes regardless of what the bird is doing at the time. He could be eating, he could be on the nest, he could be swimming, or he could even be in flight. In males, sperms are dumped out through the same all-purpose system. That is why the aft of a bird is called its cloaca, from the Latin word for "sewer." We call the all-inclusive excrement "birdshit."

When people make love we call it "billing and cooing," except for the part where the reproductive organs actually get together. We have lots of colorful terms for that. All those displays and rituals many birds perform are fine for getting a potential mate interested, but when they actually get down to doing the deed all they do is bump their cloacas together. Somehow they manage the "cloacal kiss" even with all the impediment of tail feathers and twitchy movement. It is quick, quick as a fist bump. Not very romantic. But that quick butthole bump is all that is needed for exchange of all that stuff in the excrement. The sperms swim upstream in the female to fertilize eggs. No special apparatus like vaginas and penises are involved.

Except in ducks, geese, and a few other waterfowl. Actually, the goose penis is nothing to brag about. It is really a sort of trough or groove, somewhat like the chute at the back of a cement truck that directs the flow to its target. The duck penis, though, is a bit more complicated. It is shaped like a corkscrew with several 360 turns like waterslides at waterparks. He can whip it out to its full twenty centimeter length in an instant and the term—yes, the term "screwing" applies.

Male swans also have a penis. You will probably never see one but this will give you something to think about the next time you go to the ballet to see *Swan Lake*.

If some countries have too much history, we have too much geography.
—William Lyon Mackenzie King

Billtowns

Place names don't always make sense. It is hard, for example, to see why Cincinnati is named for a Roman general, why any of the various Columbuses in the Midwest are named for a Portuguese sailor who never even knew the Midwest was *there*, or why names like Tallahassee and Mexican Hat exist at all. Names like Lover, Pillow, and Intercourse—all in Pennsylvania—conjure erotic visions hardly appropriate to images of staid gatherings of town founding fathers sitting around trying to figure out what to call their little bergs (not to worry, Pennsylvania also has a Climax.) But somehow we assume that all of the Williamsburgs, Williamsports, and the like that are scattered about North American make sense because they are named for somebody named William. Sometimes they are, but not always. The ones in the east, depending on how old they are, might be named for King William. Or they might be based on somebody's last name, like Roger Williams, the settler of Rhode Island. We can assume that the Williamports are actually ports—actually located at the side of a body of water. But even that isn't always true.

115

However they got to be called what they are, if their name starts with William-anything then they qualify for inclusion here. More than half of our fifty states have a place called Williamsburg, Williamsport, or Williamstown. Pennsylvania has all three. We can't visit them all, but we can certainly look at a few of the more colorful ones.

Let' start with a few that are darned hard to find, like **Williamsburg, New Mexico**. It is a suburb, if you can call it that when the mothertown has only 6,000 people, of a not very big place called Truth or Consequences. There can't be a dumber name than that so we can't blame a group of neighbors for protesting. Originally, the entire town was called Hot Springs, named for some smelly warm waters there that attracted tourists looking for a nice, relaxing soak. The whole name-changing affair began in 1950 when a very popular radio game show—*Truth or Consequences*—made an offer to broadcast their tenth anniversary show from the first town in America that would volunteer to change its name to the name of the program. Just think of the clamor today if someone offered to change the name of *your* town in Who Wants to Be a Millionaire? or The Bachelorette. You could actually be living or Game of Thrones, North Dakota or Wheel of Fortune, Arkansas. It is surprising that there were any takers to the offer at all.

But *Truth or Consequences* was wildly popular. It was a radio hit starting in 1940 and at some point in the '50's it morphed into TV. The concept was silly: Contestants were asked a question and they would get the answer wrong. Questions like "Who is buried in Grant's tomb?" Nobody would think of the correct answer[*] to that.

As a penalty for the wrong answer the contestant had to pay the consequences by completing a task, usually an embarrassing one. One fellow had to explain how to milk a cow in Italian to an attractive girl who didn't understand Italian. He was allowed liberal use his hands to demonstrate. There was no cow present; the girl was stacked. Another was sent home with a supply of Christmas Seals. The catch: they were live seals. Another was given a chest with a significant amount of money in it and was told that he would receive the key in the mail during the following week. The catch to that one was that everyone in America was given his address and he received thousands of keys to try one at a time.

Well, Hot Springs, New Mexico, won the challenge and agreed to change their name. But a group of neighbors on the southwest side thought it really stupid and refused to go along with it. They tried to call their little section of town Hot Springs but the name didn't stick so in 1950 they incorporated as Williamsburg, named for their mayor Thomas Williams. Williamsburg is not printed on every map and even when you go there nothing tells you that you have arrived. But it is indeed a nice, quiet neighborhood of folks who are happy to be there. They're on a little hill just above town and they can always buzz down there for a brief whiff from the hot springs when they need a sulfur fix. It's a nice place to live.

---

[*] Mr. and Mrs. Grant.

So is **Williamsburg, Colorado**. This is another wee town known not so much for the town itself as for what it is near. Which in this case is Florence, Colorado, which is near Cañon City, Colorado, which is near the Royal Gorge of the Arkansas. Which is a ferocious river. The rocks on both sides of the gorge are more than a billion years old but the gorge itself is relatively young—it was carved out by the river only five million years ago. When viewed from its brim or from the bridge that spans it, the river is a dizzying 1,250 feet below. The Empire State Building would just fit in there. For most of its five million years the gorge was a quiet, peaceful place. In the last hundred years, though, it has been anything but. That's because in 1929 a suspension bridge was built from one rim to the other. It was a bridge to nowhere. Yes, it crosses the canyon, but there is no road continuing on once you reach the other side. All you can do is turn around and walk back, peering down into the void below you on the way. More recently, somebody figured out that adrenaline sells and developed a fully-staged amusement park there—ziplines, gondolas, and the like. The whole place is designed on adrenaline. "The World's Scariest Skycoaster," a slingshot sort of contraption sends you out over the canyon at 50 miles per hour. Thankfully, it does bring you back. "America's Highest Zipline" will also take you across, as will the aerial gondola. In the kiddie area there is a carousel; for some visitors, not all of them kiddies, that is adrenaline enough. Places like this particular Williamsburg, with at least 5,000 people, are classified as "census towns." It was incorporated in 1888, well after the Colorado gold rush of 1856 and the Colorado silver boom of 1879. It was coal and gas that brought people to Williamsburg, but it's the gorge upstream that brings people through it.

Like several other lesser-known Williamsburgs, **Williamsburg, Iowa**, is interesting because of things near it. In this case that means lots of cornfields—acres and acres of them. More than 85 percent of the total acreage of Iowa is planted in corn and no state produces more corn, about 2.5 billion bushels per year, than Iowa. It is "field corn," not the sweet corn that we eat with butter and salt at backyard barbeques. Mostly it is fed to animals, used to make corn syrup, or fermented to produce ethanol.

With all that corn growing, it is not surprising that one of the principal employers in Williamsburg, Iowa, is a seed company—Holden Foundation Seeds. This is a company that has been around since 1937, now owned by Monsanto, that specializes in producing hybrid seed corn. In fact, about forty percent of the corn planted in the US started there. If you drive in either direction between, say Dayton, Ohio, and Grand Island, Nebraska, you are going to see an awful lot of corn. Most of it is Holden Foundation stuff.

The other significant phenomenon just minutes away from Williamsburg, Iowa, is a collection of seven small villages known as the Amana Colonies. Their names are not too imaginative—Middle Amana, South Amana, East Amana, West Amana, and so on.

The colonies were established in the middle of the nineteenth century, 1856 to be exact, when a group of religious settlers arrived. They had started out in Germany but emigrated to upstate New

York when persecution for their religious views became intolerable. Trouble was, they found persecution in New York as well. Hence their migration to Iowa, where the tall corn grows. They are often confused with the Amish, who had similar origins. While the Amish are more widely distributed, especially in Pennsylvania and Ohio, with smaller populations in other mostly eastern and midwestern states, the Amanas are limited to that small area of Iowa.

In their early days life was mostly communal, with shared dining, shared gardens, shared government, communal kitchens, communal laundry, and shared labor. In school the children were taught reading, writing, arithmetic, and corn—how to sort the seed, shell the ears, grade the corn, and all that. Today it is a popular spot for tourists who pull off Interstate-80 for lunch, a lookabout, and shopping. Shelves of the shops are abundantly stocked with jellies and jams, corn relish, corn muffins, corn bread, potholders shaped like ears of corn, and pretty much anything corn.

Corny? Not at all. The colonies are the real thing, nothing artificial about them at all. They are quiet reminders of yesteryear, of a time when life was close to the earth and folks relied on each other. Absolutely no adrenaline there.

Williamsburg, Pennsylvania is another Williamsburg that is not known so much for being Williamsburg, Pennsylvania, itself as for things it is near. Which in this case is a lot of pretty hills, lots of state-owned game lands, lots of lakes, and one Horseshoe Curve. The Curve is an engineering marvel famous in railroad history. When the workers at Pennsylvania Railroad were laying track in 1854 from east to west across Pennsylvania they were faced with a major barrier—the Allegheny (with a silent and superfluous *h*) Mountains. There was no way to get to Pittsburgh (there's that superfluous *h* again) without going over the mountains. They were, and still are, too steep for a train. So instead of tracking straight up the mountain they laid the track so that it ascends gradually along a giant curve around the head of a valley. It takes half a mile of track to rise only 122 feet. An engineer at the front of a reasonably long train can see his own caboose. Conductors on Amtrak's Capitol Limited trains using that track make an announcement when their train is approaching the Curve so that passengers won't miss it. Now if they would only adjust the schedule so that the Curve doesn't happen at midnight! Some people prefer sleeping to railroad history.

Williamsburg, Ohio, was established in 1852. Union. Its name was Williamsburgh, with one of those silent *h*'s on the end. The "burg" or "burgh" part of names like that comes from "borough;" a few places like Pittsburgh and Plattsburgh have, for no apparent logical reason, retained the *h*. Most places dropped it, as did Williamsburgh in1893. This Williamsburg, now without its *h*, is not far from Cincinnati and all things Cincinnati, not far from the Ohio River and all of its activity and scenery, and not far from Kings Island, which is not an island at all but one of the most-attended amusement parks in America. Like many amusement parks, this one boasts some of the highest or fastest or scariest rides on the planet. Crowds love them. Yes, adrenaline sells!

Since Kentucky is just across the river from Ohio, one might think that it is not very far from Williamsburg, Ohio, to **Williamsburg, Kentucky**. But the Kentucky one, absolutely due south of the Ohio one—they are on the same meridian—is about as far south as anyone in Kentucky can get. A few miles further south and it would be in Tennessee. It is located in the beautiful Cumberland Mountains and the Cumberland River flows through the middle of it. A few miles upstream is Cumberland Falls, where visitors can see, on full-moon nights, its famous "moonbow" in the mist below the falls. It is like a rainbow of the sort we see when the sun comes back out on rainy days or that we see in our lawn sprinklers, but it is even more awesome and sort of haunting when the light comes from the moon. Moonbows probably occur in many other waterfalls around America, like Niagara Falls and Yosemite Falls, but we do not see them because the falls either dry up much of the year or are lit up every night with colored floodlights. But the Cumberland Falls moonbow is reliable all year round. Couples have been known to plan their weddings so that they can be at the Falls during a full moon. If it happens to be cloudy that night and they can't view the moonbow, no problem; they're honeymooners, they'll just have to find some else to do.

But if a couple announces that they are going to Williamsburg for their honeymoon, chances are that they are not planning a trip to any of the Williamsburgs mentioned above—certainly not one in the middle of Iowa, southern Ohio, or central Pennsylvania. In fact, if someone mentions "Williamsburg" without a qualifying state name immediately following, then they probably are referring to their plans to go to *the* Williamsburg—**Williamsburg, Virginia**. There are actually two Williamsburgs—the town of Williamsburg itself, and an area of historic reconstruction called Colonial Williamsburg.

Williamsburg, the town in tidewater Virginia, is really old. It was established as a fort in 1638 but it was not given its current name until 1699 when the town was designated as capital of the Virginia colony and named for the reigning monarch King William III. Since the throne at the time was shared between William and his wife Mary, the place could just as well have been called Marysburg. Or Williandandmarysburg. The local college, The College of William and Mary, is named for both of them. Some families go to Williamsburg to absorb history, some go for the shopping outlets, and some go for Busch Gardens, the amusement park that sells adrenaline. Rides there have intimidating names like Battering Ram, Verboten, and Apollo's Chariot, which promises "six staggering inversions." It is not clear whether free barf bags are included in the hefty ticket price.

Other families skip all of that entirely and head directly to the visitor center for Colonial Williamsburg. This is the area of historic preservation, the "world's largest living history museum." Not only are the early buildings preserved there, but colonial ways of life are on display as well. It is pretty easy to tell which people are the costumed interpreters and which are the tourists. Just look at their shoes. The ones with buckles belong to the folks who work there.

The interpreters in their breeches or their mob caps can be seen doing 18th century activities like making cartwheels, baking scones, operating a print press, or weaving. Also, smashing flax stems to make linen, driving oxen, making paper out of rags, writing with quill pens, those sorts of things. Costumed kids are rolling hoops and tossing ribboned graces. Not just anybody can get a job there. The job description for potential applicants lists requirements such as "ability to remain flexible," and to be "conversant in the history of 18th-century Williamsburg, Colonial Virginia, the American colonies, West Africa, and the British Empire." With four hundred years of history behind them, applicants have a lot to master. Not only that, but they also need indefatigable stamina and charismatic stage presence. Their presentation has to be just as fresh its 300th time as it was on Day One. These folks are good! They know their stuff and can answer questions as routine as "where's the nearest bathroom?" or inquiries about historical facts. They are just as likely to get a question like "How many voting members were in the House of Burgesses?"[*] as "Are you wearing real underwear?" "What were the economic impacts and trade restrictions on tobacco and other commodities under William III?" or "Can you tell me if the ladies' room has running water?" The folks who get those jobs have truly earned their buckles.

---

[*] 22 when it began in 1619

There are two great days in a person's life—
the day we are born and the day we discover why.
—William Barclay

Birthday Bills

Every Bill you have ever known or heard of, assuming that he didn't hatch from an egg, had a birthday. Not one of them remembers the occasion. Statisticians tell us, sometimes through elaborate pages, screens, or blackboards filled with elaborate mathematical symbols and equations, that if there are 23 people in a room then there is a 50-50 chance that two of them have the same birthday. As an example, just for clarification without all the exponents and factorials, if an apartment building had hundreds of apartments and there was a party going on in each of them and people at those parties started comparing their birthdays with each other, then in half of those parties at least two people would share the same birthday. If the size of the gathering at each party increases to 75 people then the probability of two people in each room increases to 99.9%. Surely there must be a better party game. But to be absolutely 100% certain that two people share the same birthdate there would have to be 367 people at each party. The building manager would object, but even he would have the same birthday as at least one of the participants.

What all of this is getting at is that each one of us shares a birthdate with somebody named Bill. Some of them are A-list celebrities; others are lesser lights but had at least enough importance to get themselves into pages on the World Wide Web. You probably will not read this chapter carefully; there really is no particular reason to. But what you will do is hunt through these lists to find your own birthday and see what kind of somebody named Bill shares it with you. You might also want to scan the entire list looking at the types of careers, activities, or accomplishments that got these fellows on the list. The variety of occupations that Bills have had is in itself impressive—poets and inventors to embezzlers and murderers. You might also want to witness the vast geography of their birthplaces. Most of them are in America or England. That is to be expected since that is where the name William is most common. You would not expect a lot of baby boys to be named Bill in Thailand nor Ethiopia. A few Wilhelms and Guillermos, however, made the list.

In order to keep the list reasonably compact, only one Bill was chosen for each day of the year and the description of each Bill is limited to a single line. So if you see that the Bill on your own birthday was, say, a "poet" you will have to turn to the Web yourself to fill in the details, like what kind of stuff he wrote and when he did it. If he was a "general" you might want to see whether he was a winner or a loser. You have work to do; get started.

January

1 William Fox, of Fox Film Corporation, precursor company of 20th Century Fox and Fox News. 1879, Tolcsva, Hungary.

2 William Mills, archaeologist who excavated Ohio earthworks. 1860, Cincinnati.

3 William Tucker, first African-American born in America. 1624, Jamestown, Virginia.

4 William Colby, CIA Director under Nixon. 1920, St. Paul, Minnesota.

5 William Wills, English explorer of Australia. 1843, Devon, England.

6 William Russell, 37th Governor of Massachusetts. 1857, Cambridge.

7 William Peter Blatty, "The Exorcist" writer and filmmaker. 1928, New York.

8 William Hartwell, English "Doctor Who" actor. 1908, London.

9 Bill Schroeder, NFL wide receiver, Green Bay Packers. 1971, Eau Claire, Wisconsin.

10 William Sanderson, "Blade Runner" actor. 1914, Memphis, Tennessee.

11 William Penn, composer. 1943, Long Branch, New Jersey.

12 William Golden, musician, one of the Oak Ridge Boys. 1935, Alabama.

13 William French, Union General. 1815, Baltimore, Maryland.

14 William Whipple, Declaration signer representing New Hampshire. 1730, Kittery, Maine.

15 William Higgins, U.S. Marine captured in Lebanon, tortured, and hanged. 1945, Danville, Kentucky.

16 William Kennedy, American writer. 1928, Albany, New York.

17 Sir Bill Benyon, millionaire conservative Member of Parliament. 1930, Englefield Estate, England.

18   Bill Keller, New York Times journalist and TED editor. 1949, Palo Alto, California.

19   William Williams Keen, America's first brain surgeon. 1837, Philadelphia.

20   William Powell, rhythm and blues singer for the O'Jays. 1977, Canton, Ohio.

21   William Wrigley, of Wrigley's chewing gum. 1933, Chicago.

22   William Kidd, pirate. Executed. 1645, Greenock, Scotland

23   Sir William Stephenson, spymaster with codename "Intrepid," inspiration for James Bond character. 1897, Winnipeg, Canada.

24   William Congreve, British playwright, Restoration comedies. 1670, Bardsley, Yorkshire.

25   William Somerset Maugham, novelist. 1874, Paris, France (in the UK embassy).

26   Laurence "Bill" Cragie, first American military jet pilot. 1902, Concord, New Hampshire.

27   Kaiser Wilhelm II, last German emperor and King of Prussia. 1859, Kronprinzenpalais, Berlin.

28   William Burroughs, inventor of the adding machine. 1855, Rochester, New York.

29   William McKinley, 25th President of the United States of America. 1843, Niles, Ohio.

30   William King, soul trumpeter, Commodores founder. 1949, Birmingham, Alabama.

31   William Lualilo, King of Hawaii. 1835, Honolulu.

February

1 William Davenport, stage medium known for supernatural illusions.1841, Buffalo, New York.

2 Willie Kamm, MLB third baseman. 1900, San Francisco.

3 Wilhelm Johannsen, Danish geneticist, coined the word "gene." 1857, Helsingør, Denmark.

4 William Ainsworth, English writer. 1805, Manchester.

5 William Smellie, Scottish physician first to teach midwifery and obstetrics. 1697, Lanark, Scotland.

6 William Murphy, Nobelist physician for work on anemia. 1892, Stoughton, Wisconsin.

7 Sir William Higgins, astronomer and comet hunter. 1824m Cornhill, England.

8 William Tecumseh Sherman, Union general. 1891, Lancaster, Ohio.

9 William Henry Harrison, President #9. 1773, Berkeley Plantation, Virginia.

10 William Allen White, Pulitzer Prize journalist. 1868, Emporia, Kansas.

11 William Henry Fox Talbot, inventor of photographic calotype process. 1800, Dorset, England.

12 Bill Russell, Boston Celtics center. 1934, West Monroe, Louisiana.

13 William Shockley, American physicist, Nobelist for semiconductor. 1910, London, England.

14 Pawnee Bill, nee Gordon William Lillie, western showman. 1860, Bloomington, Illinois.

15 William Pickering, discovered moons of Saturn. 1858, Boston.

16 William Hamilton, "baseball's "sliding Billie." 1866, Newark, New Jersey.

17 William Cadbury, chocolatier. 1867, Edgbaston, England.

18   William Laurel Harris, muralist. 1870, Brooklyn, New York.

19   Wilhelm II, last king of Netherlands. 1817, Brussels, Belgium.

20   Billy Zoom, punk rock guitarist. 1948, Savanna, Illinois.

21   William Petersen, "C.S.I." TV star. 1953, Evanston, Illinois.

22   William Baunol, American economist. 1922, South Bronx, New York.

23   William Shirer, American historian and author. 1904, Chicago.

24   William Karl Grimm, of Grimm's fairy tales. 1786, Hanan, Holy Roman Empire.

25   William Foster, presidential candidate from Communist Party. 1881, Taunton, Virginia.

26   William Cody, "Buffalo Bill." 1846, Le Claire, Iowa.

27   Bill Hunter, Australian voice actor. 1940, Ballarat, Australia.

28   Willie Bobbo, jazz drummer. 1934, New York.

29   Willi Donnell Smith, designer of Williwear. 1948, Philadelphia.

March

1   Will Power, sports car racer with a great name. 1981, Toowamba, Australia.

2   William Elmer, politician. 1871, Robertsville, Missouri.

3   William Green, AFL labor leader. 1873, Coschocton, Ohio.

4   William Boyd, immunologist, recognized ABO blood types. 1903, Dearborn, Michigan.

5   William Oughtred, invented the slide rule and logarithms. 1574, Eton, England.

6   William Bell, creator of "The Young and the Restless." 1927, Chicago.

7   William Rockhill Nelson, editor and publisher, Kansas City Star. 1881, Ft. Wayne, Indiana.

8   William V, Prince of Orange. 1748, The Hague, The Netherlands.

9   William Greer, American actor, grandfather on "The Waltons." 1902, Frankfort, Indiana.

10   William Etty, British painter of nudes. 1787, York, England.

11   William Ruffin Cox, Confederate general at Antietam. 1832, Scotland Neck, North Carolina.

12   Sir William Perkin, British inventor of artificial dyes. 1838, London.

13   William Macy, screen actor. 1950, Miami, Florida.

14   Vilhelm Bjerknes, pioneer of weather forecasting. 1862, Oslo, Norway.

15   William Lamb, British Prime Minister. 1848, London.

16   William Langer, American historian. 1896, Boston.

17   Bill Roycroft, Olympic equestrian champion. 1915, Victoria, Australia.

18   William Murray, mountain climber. 1913, Clydeside, Scotland.

19   William Jennings Bryan, three-time presidential candidate and "cross of gold" orator. 1860, Salem, Illinois.

20   William Hurt, Hollywood actor. 1950, Washington, D.C..

21   Guillermo Haro, astronomer, studied red and blue stars. 1913, Mexico City.

22   William I, "Lord Melbourne," last King of Prussia. 1779, Berlin, Prussia.

23   William Smith, "Strata Smith," pioneer in geological mapping. 1769 Churchill, England.

24   William Morris, British wallpaper designer. 1834, London.

25   will.i.am, of Black-eyed Peas. 1975, Los Angeles.

26   William Westmoreland, US general in Viet Nam War. 1914, Saxon, South Carolina.

27   Wilhelm Roentgen, discovered X-rays. 1845, Lennep, Germany.

28   William Harris, "Doc H," British organist. 1863, London.

29   Billy Carter, brewer. Jimmy's brother. 1937, Plains, Georgia.

30   Bill Johnson, America's first Olympic gold alpine skier. 1960, Los Angeles.

31   William Daniels, American actor. 1927, Brooklyn.

April

1   William Harvey, discovered blood circulation. 1572, Kent, England.

2   Billy Pierce, legendary MLB pitcher. 1927, Detroit.

3   William "Boss" Tweed, corrupt politician. 1823, New York.

4   Bill "Little Billy" France, Jr., NASCAR pioneer. 1933, Washington, D.C.

5   William Reed Hornby Steer, powdered- wigged barrister. 1889, Tottenham, England.

6   William Branham, faith healer. 1909, Cumberland, Kentucky.

7   William Wordsworth, British poet. 1770, Cockermouth, England.

8   William Williams, Signer from Connecticut. 1731, Lebanon, Connecticut.

9   William Pee, linguist, studied Germanic languages. 1903, Bruges, Belgium.

10   William Booth, preacher, founded the Salvation Army. 1829, Sneinton, England.

11   William Campbell, astronomer and spectroscopist. 1862, Hancock, Ohio.

12   Bill Bryden, British theatre director. 1942, Greenock, England.

13   Bill Conti, Hollywood composer. 1942, Providence, Rhode Island.

14   William Dorn, congressman. 1916, Greenwood, South Carolina.

15   William Cullen, Scottish medical professor, invented artificial refrigeration. 1710, Hamilton, England.

16   Bill Belicheck, coached New England Patriots through four Super Bowls. 1952, Nashville, Tennessee.

17   William Holden, 50's Hollywood heartthrob. 1918, O'Fallon, Illinois.

18 William Sudderth, trumpet player. 1950, White Plains, New York.

19 William Axt, Hollywood composer. 1888, New York.

20 Bill Dollar, America's first *danseur noble*. 1907, East St. Louis, Illinois.

21 William Stang, anti-dancing, anti-divorce Catholic bishop. 1854, Langenbrucken, Germany.

22 William Morris, Union general, invented eight-cartridge firearm. 1827, New York.

23 J.M.W. Turner, "William Turner," British painter. 1775, London.

24 William I, "William the Silent." 1533, Dillenberg, Germany.

25 William Brennan, Jr., liberal Supreme Court justice. 1906, Newark, New Jersey.

26 (baptism date) William Shakespeare, playwright and poet. 1564, Stratford-upon-Avon, England.

27 Willem Alexander, king of The Netherlands1967, Utrecht, The Netherlands.

28 William "Wild Bill" Guarnere, WWII soldier in the "Band of Brothers." 1923, Philadelphia.

29 Willie Nelson, country music legend. 1933, Abbott, Texas.

30 Bill clay, longtime congressman form Missouri. 1931, St. Louis.

May

1 William Steel, Confederate general. 1819, Albany, New York.

2 William Bayliss, discovered peristalsis. 1860, Wolverhampton, England.

3 William Inge, Pulitzer-winning playwright. 1913, Independence, Kansas.

4 Billy O'Donnell, harness racing driver. 1948, Springhill, Nova Scotia.

5 William McTell, ragtime's "Blind Willie." 1898, Thompson, Georgia.

6 William Simmons, KKK founder. 1880, Harpersville, Alabama.

7   William Comstock, "Billy House" comedian. 1889, Mankato, Minnesota.

8   Bill Cowher, Steelers coach. 1957, Crafton, Pennsylvania.

9   William Moulton Marston, invented the lie detector, created Wonder Woman. 1893, Saugus, Massachusetts.

10 Sir William Lithgow, billionaire shipbuilder. 1934, Glasgow, Scotland.

11 William Glasser, psychiatrist, developer of reality therapy and choice theory. 1925, Cleveland.

12 William "Doc" Ewing, oceanic seismologist. 1906, Lockney, Texas.

13 William Garland, "Red Garland" jazz pianist. 1923, Dallas.

14 William Emerson, mathematician, developed wind-powered vehicle. 1701, Hurworth, England.

15 Bill Williams, TV's Kit Carson. 1915, Brooklyn, New York.

16 William Seward, Alaska purchaser ("Seward's Folly.) 1801, Florida, New York.

17 William Bruford, jazz drummer. 1949, Kent, England.

18 Bill Macy, TV husband on "Maude." 1922, Revere, Massachusetts.

19 William Gregory, paleontologist specializing in teeth. 1876, New York.

20 William Thornton, designed U.S. Capitol. 1759, Jost Van Dyke, British Virgin Islands.

21 Willem Einthoven, developed the electrocardiogram. 1860, Semarang, Java.

22 William Drake, wide receiver. 1950, Portland, Oregon.

23 William Barr, Attorney General under Trump. 1950, New York.

24 William Gilbert, discovered magnetism. 1544, Colchester, England.

25 Bill Robinson, "Bojangles" tap dancer. 11878, Richmond, Virginia.

26 Billy Downes, golfer. 1966, Camden, New Jersey.

27 James Butler Hickok, "Wild Bill Hickok." 1837, Troy Grove, Illinois.

28　William Pitt the Younger, England's youngest Prime Minister. 1759, Kent, England.

29　Willem Holleeder Heineken, extortionist. 1958, Amsterdam, The Netherlands.

30　Sir William McMurdo, British general in Crimean War. 1819, London.

31　William Lee, Confederate general, son of Robert E. 1837, Arlington, Virginia.

June

1　William Sloane Coffin, out-spoken pacifist and civil rights activist. 1924, New York.

2　William Lawson, explorer of Australia. 1774, Middlesex, England.

3　Sir William Matthews Flinders Petrie, Egyptologist. 1853, London.

4　William Batten, New York Stock Exchange chief. 1909, Reedy, Virginia.

5　Bill Moyers, of Bill Moyers News Journal. 1934, Hugo, Oklahoma.

6　William Cosgrave, President of Ireland. 1880, Dublin.

7　Bill Koch, cross-country skier. 1955, Brattleboro, Vermont.

8　William Calley, war criminal in My Lai Massacre. 1943, Miami, Florida.

9　Billy Hatton, rock star. 1941, Liverpool, England.

10　William Harris, builder of submarine docks. 1912, Liverpool, England.

11　William Styron, novelist. 1925, Newport News, Virginia.

12　Willie Horton, convicted of murder, rape, armed robbery, and assault—a political football in the 1988 Bush/Gore campaign. 1951, Chesterfield, South Carolina.

13　William Butler Yeats, poet. 1865, Sandymount, Ireland.

14　Willie Beamon, NFL quarterback. 1970, Belle Glade, Florida.

15　Billy Martin, punk keyboardist. 1981, Annapolis, Maryland.

16 Willi Boskovsky, Vienna New Year's Eve conductor. 1909, Vienna, Austria.

17 William Crookes, English chemist and physicist. 1832, London.

18 William Lassell, discovered planetary satellites. 1799, Bolton, England.

19 William Webb, shipbuilder. 1816, New York.

20 William Bealchin, geographer, with special interest in coastlines1916, Aldershot, England.

21 Prince William, Duke of Cambridge. Son of Diana. 1982, London.

22 Billy Wilder, Hollywood filmmaker. 1906, Sucha Beskidzka, Poland.

23 William Ernest Johnson, logician. 1899, Cambridge, England.

24 Billy Casper, golfer. 1931, San Diego.

25 William Potts, "Whipper Billy Watson," heavyweight wrestler. 1915, East York, Ontario.

26 William Simmons, ex-slave, later college president. 1849, Charleston, South Carolina.

27 Willie Mosconi, pool pro. 1913, Philadelphia.

28 William Hooper, Signer for North Carolina. 1742, Boston, Massachusetts.

29 William Mayo, of the Mayo Clinic. 1939, LeSeur, Minnesota.

30 Willie Sutton, bank robber and prison escapee. 1901, Brooklyn.

July

1 William Strunk, influential grammarian. 1869, Cincinnati.

2 William Bragg, X-ray crystallographer. 1862, Wigton, England.

3 William Roll, poltergeist investigator. 1926, Bremen, Germany.

4 William Rush, first major American sculptor. 1756, Philadelphia.

5 William Rankine, thermodynamics physicist. 1820, Edinburgh, Scotland.

6 Bill Haley, of Bill Haley and the Comets. 1925, Highland Park, Michigan.

7   William Feller, probability theorist. 1906, Zagreb, Croatia.

8   Billy Crudup, actor. 1968, Manhasset, New York.

9   William Waldegrave, Governor of Newfoundland. 1753, London.

10 William Blackstone, jurist, judge, and writer. 1723, London.

11 William Grove, developed first fuel cell. 1811, Swansea, Wales.

12 Bill Cosby, comedian. 1937, Philadelphia.

13 Bill Moor, actor. 1937, Toledo, Ohio.

14 William Hannah, animator of Tom and Jerry. 1910, Melrose, New Mexico.

15 William Fare, TV producer. 1949, Johannesburg, South Africa.

16 Will Farrell, comedian. 1967, Irvine, California.

17 Bill Monroe, public affairs journalist. 1920, New Orleans.

18 William Thackeray, satirist. 1811, Calcutta, India.

19 William Scranton, Pennsylvania Governor. 1917, Madison, Connecticut.

20 William Deering, pole vaulter. 1921, South Bend, Indiana.

21 Bill Taylor, hard bop musician. 1921, Greenville, North Carolina.

22 William Spooner, original speaker of spoonerisms. 1844, London.

23 William Whittaker, musicologist. 1876, Newcastle upon Tyne, England.

24 William Poole, "Bill the Butcher" in New York gangs. 1821, Sussex County, New Jersey.

25 Billy Wagner, MLB pitcher. 1971, Marion, Virginia.

26 Bill Shepherd, astronaut. 19949, Oak Ridge, Tennessee.

27 Billy Grimes, halfback. 1927, County Line, Oklahoma.

28 Bill Bradley, basketballer and US senator. 1943, Crystal City, Missouri.

29 Bill Forsyth, film director. 1946, Glasgow, Scotland.

30 William Atherton, leading man actor. 1947, Orange, Connecticut.

31 William Bennett, America's first drug czar. 1943, Brooklyn, New York.

August

1   William Clark, of Lewis and Clark. 1770, Ladysmith, Virginia.

2   William Williams, Connecticut Signer. 1731, Lebanon, Connecticut.

3   William Miller, Confederate general born in Yankeeland. 1820, Ithaca, New York.

4   Sir William Hamilton, inventor of quaternions. 1805, Dublin, Ireland.

5   Billy Bob Thornton, movie star. 1955, Hot Springs, Arkansas.

6   Sir William Sim, British general in World War II. 1891, Bishopton, England.

7   Bill Thomas, NFL backfielder. 1949, Ossining, New York.

8   William Bateson, coined the term "genetics." 1861, Whitby, England.

9   William Morton, first dentist to use ether. 1819, Charlton, Massachusetts.

10   William Howe, British general who captured Philadelphia. 1729, Twickenham, England.

11   Will Friedle, comedian. 1976, Hartford, Connecticut.

12   Willie Horton, murderer and rapist. 1951, Chesterfield, South Carolina.

13   William Bernbach, ad slogans creator. 1911, New York.

14   William Hutchinson, magistrate of early Rhode Island settlement. 1586, Alford, England.

15   Willie Pinkney, of The Drifters. 1925, Daizell South Carolina.

16   William Maxwell, New Yorker editor. 1908, Lincoln, Illinois.

17   William Mark Felt, Watergate's "Deep Throat." 1913, Twin Falls, Idaho.

18   William Rushton, satirist, cartoonist, all-round wit. 1937, London.

19   Bill Clinton, #42. 1946, Hope, Arkansas.

20   William Buckner, Olympic hoopster. 1954, Phoenix.

21   William IV, the "Sailor King." 1765, Buckingham Palace, London.

22 Bill Parcells, "The Big Tuna," NFL coach. 1941, Englewood, New Hampshire.

23 Will Cuppy, humorist. 1884, Auburn, Indiana.

24 William Wilberforce, influential British abolitionist. 1759, Kingston upon Hull, England.

25 Billy Ray Cyrus, singer with an Achy, Breaky Heart. 1961, Flatwoods, Kentucky.

26 Will Shortz, crossword puzzle guru. 1952, Crawfordsville, Indiana.

27 Billy Buckner, pitcher. 1983, Decatur, Georgia.

28 Billy Grammer, of Grand Ole Opry. 1925, Benton, Illinois.

29 Wilhelm Pachelbel, composer of *Canon in D*. 1686, Erfurt, Germany.

30 Willie Bryant, "Mayor of Harlem," jazz musician. 1908, Chicago.

31 William Wells, Bombadier," heavyweight boxer. 1889, London.

September

1 Billy Blanks, karate guru. 1955, Erie, Pennsylvania.

2 William Sommerville, sports poet. 1675, Warren, England.

3 Bill Flemming, sports journalist. 1926, Chicago.

4 William Lyons, of Jaguar cars. 1901, Blackpool, England.

5 William Dampier, first pirate to circumnavigate the globe three times. 1651 Somerset, England.

6 William Rosencrans, "Old Rosie," Union general, invented a method to make soap. 1819, Kingston, Ohio.

7 William Friese Greene, developed motion picture process. 1855, Bristol, England.

8 William Law, founder of True Church of Jesus Christ of Latter Day Saints. 1809, County Tyrone, Ireland.

9   William Bligh, captain of The Bounty. 1754, Plymouth, England.

10 Bill O'Reilly, "Money Guy," journalist. 1949, New York.

11 William Porter, "O Henry," short story writer. 1862, Greensboro, North Carolina.

12 William Dugdale, Garter King of Arms. 1605, Shustoke, England.

13 Bill Monroe, "Father of Bluegrass." 1911, Rosine, New York.

14 William Ayrton, physics of telegraphy, developed method to fix lines. 1847, London.

15 William H. Taft, #27. 1857, Cincinnati.

16 William Johnston, Church of Scotland Moderator. 1921, Edinburg.

17 William Bonney, "Billy the Kid." 1859, New York.

18 Guillermo Vargas, "Habacuc," cruel artist. 1957, San Jose, Costa Rica.

19 William Golding, writer, Lord of the Flies. 19911, Newquay, England.

20 William Illingworth, stereophotographer at Custer's Last Stand. 1844, Leeds, England.

21 Billy Murray, actor. 1950, Evanston, Illinois.

22 Bilbo Baggins, hobbit and burglar. 1290, Middle Earth.

23 William McGuffey, educator, published reading primers. 1800, Claysville, Pennsylvania.

24 William Adams, first western samurai. 1564, Gillingham, England.

25 Will Smith, Newsweek's "most powerful actor in Hollywood." 1966, Philadelphia.

26 Bill France Sr., founder of NASCAR. 1909, Washington, D.C.

27 William Orr, producer of prime-time hits and TV westerns. 1917, New York.

28 Billy Montana, country music singer-songwriter. 1959, Voorheesville, New York.

29 Bill Nelson, astronaut. 1942, Miami, Florida.

30 William Stoughton, judge at Salem witch trials. 1631, Dorchester, Massachusetts.

October

1 William Boeing, aircraft company founder. 1881, Detroit.

2 Sir William Ramsey, discovered inert gasses. 1852, Glasgow, Scotland.

3 William Gorgas, yellow fever control. 1854, Toulminville, Alabama.

4 William Griggs, developed lithography process. 1832, Woburn, England.

5 Willi Unsoeld, first American up Mt. Everest. 1926, Arcata, California.

6 William Butler, indie rocker. 1982, The Woodlands, Texas.

7 William Billings, first American hymnologist. 1746, Boston.

8 Will Vodery, first African-American Broadway composer. 1885, Philadelphia.

9 William McAnulty, first Black justice on Kentucky Supreme Court. 1947, Indianapolis.

10 Willie Davis, wide receiver. 1967, Little Rock, Arkansas.

11 William Sledd, "Ask a Gay Man" video, blogger. 1983, Paducah, Kentucky.

12 William Raspberry, columnist. 1935, Okalona, Mississippi.

13 Billy Bush, TV host. 1971, New York.

14 William Penn, Quaker founder of Pennsylvania. 1644, London.

15 Willie O'Ree, first Black NHL player. 1935, Fredericton, New Brunswick.

16 William Douglas, supreme Court justice. 1898, Maine Township, Minnesota.

17 William "Candy" Cummings, invented the curve ball. 1848, Ware, Massachusetts.

18 Willie Horton, left fielder for six MLB teams. 1942, Arno, Virginia.

19 William Cheselden, wrote first anatomy book in English. 1688, Somerset, England.

20 Will Rogers, actor, commentator, wit. 1920, New York.

21 Will Estes, TV cop. 1978, Los Angeles.

22 William V, Duke of Aquitaine, earliest troubadour. 1071, Aquitaine, France.

23 William Thomas Turner, captain of the RMS Lusitania. 1856, Liverpool, Engand.

24 William Dobelle, artificial vision restored sight to blind patients. 1941, Pittsfield, Massachusetts.

25 William Higinbotham, physicist on first atomic bomb project. 1910, Bridgeport, Connecticut.

26 William Vanderbilt, rich guy. 1878, New York.

27 William Maclure, first geological map. 1763, Ayr, Scotland.

28 Bill Gates, 90X billionaire, philanthropist. 1955, Seattle.

29 Bill Maudlin, WWII cartoonist. 1921, Mountain Park, New Mexico.

30 William Sumner, social scientist and libertarian. 1849, Patterson, New Jersey

31 William Paca, Maryland signer. 1740, Abington, Maryland.

November

1 Willie D, hip hopper. 1966, Houston, Texas.

2 Bill Johnston, "Little Bill," tennis champ. 1894, San Francisco.

3 William Cullen Bryant, transcendental poet. 1794, Cummington, Massachusetts.

4 William III, "William of Orange." 1650, Binnenhof, The Netherlands.

5 Bill Walton, NBA sportscaster. 1952, La Mesa, California.

6   Bill Henderson, guitarist. 1944, Vancouver, British Columbia.

7   Billy Graham, evangelist. 1918, Charlotte, North Carolina.

8   William Robertson Smith, Semitic scholar. 1846, Kieg, Scotland.

9   Bill Mantlo, writer for Marvel Comics. 1951, Brooklyn, New York.

10   William Hogarth, British engraver and social satirist. 1697, London.

11   Billy Smith, country singer. 1956, Reidsville, North Carolina.

12   William Davies, "Pennar Davies," Welsh author. 1911, Mountain Ash, Wales.

13   Billy Klüver, Bell Labs engineer. 1927, Monaco.

14   William Darrow, Union general. 1822, Winchester, Kentucky.

15   William Pitt the Elder, influential Whig. 1708, Westminster, England.

16   W.C. Handy, "Father of the Blues." 1873, Florence, Alabama.

17   Bill McCreary, hockey referee. 1955, Guelph, Ontario.

18   William Gilbert, of Gilbert and Sullivan. 1836, London.

19   Billy Sunday, athlete, evangelist, and prohibitionist. 1862, Ames, Iowa.

20   William Painter, invented bottle cap and bottle cap opener. 1838, Ireland.

21   William Beaumont, stomach physiologist. 1785, Lebanon, Connecticut.

22   Billy Sprague, rocket scientist. 1953, Fort Collins, Colorado.

23   William FitzAlan, 16th Earl of Arundel, and 6th Baron Maltravers. 1417, Arundel, England.

24   William Ellis, preacher and inventor of rugby football. 1804, Salford, England.

25   Bill Morrissey, folksinger. 1951, Hartford, Connecticut.

26   Bill Wilson, founded Alcoholics Anonymous. 1895, East Dorset, Vermont.

27   Bill Nye, the "Science Guy." 1955, Washington, D.C.

28   William Blake, British poet. 1727, London.

29   Billy Stayhorn, pianist and composer, "Take the A Train." 1915, Dayton, Ohio.

30   William Broad, "Billy Idol," musician. 1955, Stanmore, England.

December

1   Billy Childish, garage punk rocker. 1959, Chatham, England.

2   William Ellery, Signer from Rhode Island. 1727, Newport, Rhode Island.

3   Bill Steer, heavy metal guitarist. 1969, Stockton-on-Tees, England.

4   William Alexander, "Lord Stirling." General under George Washington. 1726, New York.

5   Bill Pickett, rodeo cowboy. 1871, Jenks Branch, Texas.

6   William II, King of the Netherlands. 1792, The Hague.

7   William Procter, of Procter and Gamble. 1801, Herefordshire, England.

8   Bill Bryson, humorist and keen observer. 1951, Des Moines, Iowa.

9   Bill Hartack, five-time Kentucky Derby winner. 1932, Ellensburg, Pennsylvania.

10   William Garrison, founded American Anti-Slavery Society. 1805, Newburyport, Massachusetts.

11   William Kilgore, Patty Hearst's kidnapper. 1947, Portland, Oregon.

12   William Vanderbilt, richest American of his day. 1849, Staten Island, NewYork.

13   Bill Castro, MLB coach and pitcher. 1953, Santiago, Dominican Republic.

14   William "Carrot Top" Wells, Indian agent, captain in War of 1812. 1770, Jacob's Creek, Pennsylvania.

15   William Hitzig, New York physician who aided Hiroshima victims. 1904, Austria.

16   William Perry, "The Refrigerator," in NFL. 1962, Aiken, South Carolina.

17   William Floyd, Signer from New York. 1734, Brookhaven, New York.

18   Willy Brandt, West German Chancellor. 1913, Lübeck, Germany.

19   William DeVries, developed first artificial heart. 1943, Brooklyn, New York.

20 Billy Bragg, singer and leftwing activist. 1957, Barking, England.

21 Willi Resetarits, Austrian comedian and singer. 1948, Stinatz, Austria.

22 Bill Lipinski, Congressman. 1937, Chicago.

23 Bill Rodgers, four-time winner of Boston Marathon. 1947, Hartford, Connecticut.

24 William Patterson, Signer of the Constitution. 1754, Antrim, Ireland.

25 William Moffett, architect of pre-fab concrete hexagonal houses. 1912, Cork, Ireland.

26 Willie Williams, NFL cornerback. 1970, Columbia, South Carolina.

27 William Masters, sex author. 1915, Cleveland.

28 William Chilton, songwriter, lead singer of the Box Tops and Big Star. 1950, Memphis, Tennessee.

29 William Bridgeman, Home Secretary, cricketeer, and first Viscount Bridgeman. 1864, London.

30 William Barrett, existentialist philosopher. 1913, New York.

31 William Bridgeman, cricketeer, Home Secretary, and first Viscount Bridgeman. 1864, Leigh, England.

Acknowledgments, comments, etc.

It is pretty obvious by now that this is not a scholarly opus. It was never intended to be, so there is no lengthy Literature Cited section to credit sources for all of the detailed facts and trivia herein. Most of it came from Googling the internet. Wikipedia is trustworthy enough for a project such as this. Some really useful websites for the epigraphs are brainyquote.com and bartlettsquotes.com. For birthdays a good place to start is on-this-day.com. But a word of caution: surfing about for stuff like kings named William or odd facts about birds is highly subject to distraction. What might be expected to be a quick fact-checking mission can lead to hours of entertaining attention to things entirely unrelated. It's like looking something up in an illustrated dictionary— remember dictionairies?—and spending half an hour on everything else on that page.

Under no circumstances should anything from these pages ever be cited as an authority itself in any other publication. The few printed sources used have been cited in the text unless they were handouts picked up in museums and tourist bureaus. Anyone wanting to verify those can go there themselves. Have a good trip.

Thanks to Lee, my advisor for Word and, for that matter, everything else in my life except for spelling and directions. She is clearly the best thing ever conceived in Panama. Thanks to Pat Achilles for the cover art and to Comma King Joe.

Greatest thanks of all to everyone who has a brother-in-law, a nephew, or a co-worker named Bill and got them a copy of this because they couldn't think of anything else remotely appropriate. If you fall into that category, just remember that payback is hell. That Bill in your life might get even.

Printed in the United States
by Baker & Taylor Publisher Services